REASONS FOR THE SEASONS

Reasons for the Seasons

Origins of the Christian Holidays

JASON HUNT, PH.D.

Barefoot Prophet Media

Contents

Introduction ix

1. Pagan Origins 1
2. The Origins of Easter 10
3. Easter Revolution 15
4. Rites of Passage 21
5. The Spring Festivals 32
6. The Day of Resurrection 39
7. Christmas Origins 43
8. Deck the Halls 54
9. What about Santa Claus? 64
10. The Invincible Sun 71

11	Prophecy Fulfilled	76
12	The Fall Festivals	81
13	So, What now?	86

References   97
About the Author   109

Copyright © 2010, 2012, 2021 by Jason A. Hunt

All rights reserved. No part of this book may be reproduced in any manner whatsoever without written permission except in the case of brief quotations embodied in critical articles and reviews.

Third Printing, 2021

Cover Background: Photo by Laura James from Pexels

ISBN/SKU 978-0-578-90385-9
EISBN 978-1-0879-6377-8

Introduction

The Lord restored my wife's womb!

After having three children, my wife Robyn began having miscarriages. We wanted to have a large family, but this setback was not only challenging due to the loss of life- but the after-effects on Robyn's physical condition. After the first miscarriage, we went to the hospital, not understanding the whole process; they explained it to us and then said they wanted to keep Robyn overnight to perform a "D&C"[1]. We waived the offer to stay and have the procedure done, and they attempted to force her to stay, at which time we walked out, for we know the Lord is our healer. After another week, she returned to normal, and all was well.

Several months later, she conceived again. A couple of months into that pregnancy, another miscarriage took place- we prayed, fasted, prophesied, but it still happened; this time, the bleeding continued way past the typical time frame. One month, then two, then three, then four! Some may think that it's just plain stupid not to go to the "doctor" to get checked out, but when you are dead broke and have no insurance, you're left with little option. A good month would provide us with about $1000 in total income at this point in our lives. Full-time ministry is difficult.

In New Testament times; either God healed them, or they opted to go to a healer, which often was no better than just staying at home to heal on your own; these things just went on (Luke 8:43-48), it's still like that today in 90% of the modern world, we take it for granted here in the West. So, we continued by faith; during the fourth month, which was in the Spring, we decided to celebrate the Biblical Holidays. We were quickly coming upon Passover and needed to prepare. We had known of the Biblical Holidays for some time but had not yet made the word come alive in our life; we knew that now was the time to act. We celebrated Passover and began preparing to celebrate the Feast of Unleavened Bread, it was the night before the Feast, and it was during our scripture study that evening when Robyn shouted, "I got it!" this is what she found:

Exodus 23:25-26 (NKJV): "So you shall serve the LORD your God, and He will bless your bread and your water. And I will take sickness away from the midst of you. No one shall suffer miscarriage or be barren in your land; I will fulfill the number of your days."

This verse identifies a promise God gave to those that kept the feasts (Ex. 23:14-24). It was then that we knew she would be healed- and four days into the Feast of Unleavened Bread, the bleeding stopped, and she regained her health. Fourth months later, she again started to have signs of another miscarriage. It scared us for a moment, so we became indignant and stood on the fact that God healed her during the Feast of Unleavened Bread. Heavy bleeding subsided a few days later, which is when she could get another doctor's appointment. The doctor tried to affirm the worst as they could not locate a heartbeat or any evidence a baby was viable in the womb; the doctor left the room for a time. Upon returning, she asked Robyn if she would like a second exam with ultrasound, to which she agreed, and sure enough, there it was- a baby.

As I update this book for the third time, Praise the Lord, our son "Daniel Asher" is thirteen years old. My purpose in writing this text is to demonstrate the pervasive Pagan origins of the church holidays of Easter and Christmas and note how all other holidays on the modern church calendar are also entirely unbiblical. Secondly, I seek to bring to light the holidays of the Lord the church is to celebrate, along with several reasons we should and how these special days reveal God's plan of preparedness for His Bride, the Church.

I do not seek to muddy your spiritual water with a message of condemnation. Still, I strive to build you up through the truths revealed in the following pages only to get you to love Jesus more than the artificial traditions we've all entertained in our ignorance. *You are about to learn things that go against the grain of 1700+ years of traditional church teaching!* So, prepare to have your mind renewed unto the word of God (Rom. 12:2).

Hosea 4:6 states that God's people die due to a lack of knowledge because they reject it, and because they reject it, He shall reject them from becoming His priests.

Plainly stated, to reject the truth is to deny the Messiah Jesus himself, for He is truth (John 14:6). People are dying because they refuse to be obedient to the Biblical message. Christians are to be set apart from the world of darkness (Eph. 5:11) and the traditions of men (Mark 7). To "learn not the way of the heathen" (Jer. 10:2); "Abstain from all appearance of evil." (1 Thessalonians 5:22), to name only a few! Why then do Christians contend against any teaching that reveals the truth of the pagan nature of their beloved holidays?

In general, people fear and do not accept change, though they believe they want it. However, actions speak louder than words. Common excuses among Christians range from "*Well I didn't know...*", to "*I know, but my church teaches this...*", "*Yes, but God knows my heart...*", and the most deceived comment of all "*I know, but my church and family celebrates Jesus during this time, unlike others...*"

One author on 'Radical Church Reform' states, *"Our spiritual forefathers chose to compete with the pagans by redeeming certain days for Jesus Christ that had traditionally been kept sacred by their heathen neighbors. The Christians chose those same days to honor their Lord instead of going along with the pagan celebrations. It was a testimony against paganism and a way to "redeem the days." I find nothing wrong with this at all."*[3]

This view is the most commonly taught and accepted by the majority of churches today. However, this view is grossly flawed because these "Christian forefathers" were not concerned with the Christianity preached by Jesus and the Apostles- they were primarily concerned with gaining power over the people to expand the Roman church's influence. These supposed "Christian Forefathers" were all of a pagan background and were Anti-Semites (Anti-Jewish). The Christians were initially considered a sect of Judaism, just like the Pharisees or Essenes. It wasn't until the Council of Nicaea that Christianity became an independent religion, which was over 300 years after the resurrection. This Romanized Christianity took the same methods, symbolism, and dates of the old pagan festival days they had always celebrated and ascribed a saint's name to them in their effort to redeem them "for Christ."

Here remains the problem; nothing changed but the title of the day! Additionally, you will find no Biblical precedent for the redeeming of days, nor will you find any mention of our supposedly redeemed 'Christian' holiday celebrations in the bible.[2]

We hear so often to "*Keep Christ in Christmas*," the thing is, Jesus never had anything to do with Christmas! If days are not in the bible, shouldn't we stop trying to base them on biblical truth? When we look at the true nature and often the original name of the festival our Christian holiday supposedly redeemed, we find it throughout the scriptures with the command to rebuke, reprove and turn away from it. A name change isn't enough to justify a practice of a holiday dedicated to an idol.

This same author on "*Radical Church Reform*" further goes on to state: "*How, why, and when God's people remember and celebrate the birth, death, and resurrection of Jesus*

Christ is a matter of personal conscience (Romans 14:1-6). Therefore, I have never had a burden to address these things. I stand with Paul, who was a non-legalist, in his conclusion about observing certain days: "Let every man be persuaded in his own mind."[4]

Would it be okay for someone to celebrate your birthday whenever they chose? They didn't bother to ask you, and they left the celebration of your birth up to their conscience; they even had all their friends agree that they would celebrate your birth on a day they chose for you. They've convinced themselves that March is a better time to celebrate your September birthday. Then, when they celebrate "your day," they buy gifts for themselves and their family, but not you. They have a party but don't invite you, and they decorate, but not with anything you appreciate or value. Does this make sense? Of course not, yet this is what over a billion people do every year in the name of "Christ." This celebration is a simple illustration of taking God's name in vain.

In Romans 14:1-6, Paul spoke about food and fasting, what to eat during those fast days, etc., and not holidays in general. Paul stated that there was no difference regarding which Sabbath days we chose to fast on or what we decided to fast from; one day is not holier than another for fasting purposes. The concern was not judging the person who was not fasting when you were and not eating what you were eating. This concept is self-evident when reading the rest of the chapter in context.

When to celebrate the birth, death and resurrection are outlined in scripture and how to do so. So, to leave it as a matter of "personal conscience" leads one to honor the idols they've created in their heart. The Lord has made it clear; there is a way to worship Him and a way not to worship Him. My mission in this text is to unveil the truth behind the history of our holidays, unveil the pagan gods Christians are praising, and give the Biblical record for holidays we're Biblically commanded to celebrate, yes, even as Gentile Christians.

Jason Hunt, Ph.D.
Bethlehem, Kentucky
Passover 2021

Chapter 1

Pagan Origins

To the ordinary public and average Christian, the connection between Paganism and Christianity is relatively remote. The common notion is that Christianity was a miraculous disruption of the old world order; that the pagan gods fled away in dismay before the sign of the Cross and at the sound of the name of Jesus. This view was and remained encouraged by the institutional church to enhance its authority and importance; yet, it is pretty misleading and contrary to the facts that every serious Bible student knows well.

The majority of Christian traditions and festivals are directly derived from, and related to, preceding idol and nature worships. Through a great deal of storytelling and falsification, this great deception has largely remained out of sight.[1]

At Jesus' time and for hundreds of years before, the Mediterranean world had been the scene of many pagan creeds and rituals. There were scores of Temples dedicated to gods great and small, ranging from Apollo and Dionysus among the Greeks, Mithras in Persia, Adonis and Tammuz in Syria with Attis in Phrygia, and Osiris, Isis, and Horus in Egypt. Baal and Astarte were found among the Babylonians and Carthaginians, and so on.

The gods united ancient societies in service with the ceremonies and holy days. Extraordinarily interesting is that notwithstanding great geographical distances and racial differences between the adherents of these various cults and differences in the details of their services, the general outlines of their creeds and ceremonies were, if not identical so similar it is incredible. Roughly all or nearly all of the deities above mentioned believed about their god[2]:

1. They were born near Christmas Day.
2. They were born of a Virgin-Mother.
3. They were birthed in a Cave or Underground Chamber.
4. They led a life of toil for humanity.
5. They were called Healer, Mediator, Savior, and Deliverer.
6. They descended into Hell or an Underworld.
7. They rose from the dead and became the pioneers of mankind to the Heavenly world.
8. They founded communities of followers into which various styles of Baptism received disciples.

9. And they were commemorated by Festivals typically celebrating their birth as an annual tradition.

How did so many cultures space so far apart hold such similar beliefs? The Tower of Babel is the definitive Biblical answer. As you may recall, all the people of the world spoke one language and knew of only one God at one time, that is, before they decided to build a tower. When the Spirit of the Lord confused the languages of man, it caused men to spread into different areas of the land, thus resulting in other nations, tribes, people, and languages. This convolution is why the ancient people in Mexico have the same flood stories as those in Egypt and Persia. So, ancient people utilized the same stories to create new religious systems and beliefs, all straying from what God originally intended.

For the sake of further understanding, allow me to give a few brief examples.

Mithras was born in a cave on the 25th of December.[3] He was born of a Virgin.[4] He traveled far and wide as a teacher and illuminator of men. He slew the Divine Bull (a symbol of the entire earth/humanity), and his primary festivals are the winter solstice and spring equinox. He had twelve companions (the twelve months) and was buried in a tomb, from which he rose. Followers celebrated this resurrection annually with great rejoicing. He was called savior and mediator and shown as a lamb in some artistic renderings. His followers held sacramental feasts in remembrance of him.

According to the Greek historian and philosopher Plutarch, Osiris was born on the 27th of December. As King of Egypt, he taught men civility and "tamed them by music and gentleness, not by force of arms";[5] he was the discoverer of corn and wine. He was betrayed by the power of darkness, Typhon, and slain and dismembered. "His death happened," says Plutarch, "on the 17th day of the month Athyr, when the sun enters into the Scorpion." (This is the sign of the Zodiac which indicates the oncoming of winter). His body was put in a box, but three days later came back to life, as in the cults of Mithras, Dionysus, Adonis, and others. Annually, an effigy was placed in a coffin and was brought out before the adherents of the cult and was saluted with cries of "Osiris is risen, his sufferings, death, and his resurrection were enacted year by year in a great mystery play at Abydos."[6] (Much like the Passion plays of today)

The following cultic myths are more agricultural and rely less upon the cosmological signs.

Tammuz (aka Adonis), the Syrian god of vegetation, was a handsome youth born of virgin Nature. He was so handsome that Venus and Proserpine (the goddesses of the upper and underworlds) fell in love with him. To reconcile their claims of love, he would have to spend half the year in the upper world (summer) and half with Proserpine in the underworld (winter). He was killed by a wild boar (Typhon) in the autumn. And every year, the maidens "wept for Tammuz" (see Ezekiel 8:14). As flora and fauna rebirthed in the spring, a festival of his resurrection was held. The women set out to seek him. Having found the supposed corpse, place it (an idol) in a small coffin or hollowed tree and performed wild rites and lamentations, followed by even more tumultuous rejoicings over his supposed resurrection.

Some adherents would sojourn to Aphaca in the North of Syria, where a famous grove and temple resided. The Temple of Astarte (See Judges 6:25; Astarte is the Greek spelling of Easter), near a wild woodland full of trees, the birthplace of the river Adonis. The area was identified by water rushing from a cavern under lofty cliffs; here (it was said) every year, the youth Adonis/Tammuz was annually wounded to death, and the river would run red with his blood.[7] There was a scarlet anemone (a flower) that bloomed among the cedars and walnuts in this region.

The story of Attis is also very similar. He was a fair young shepherd Phrygia, beloved by Cybele, the Mother of the gods. He was born of a Virgin (Nana) who conceived by putting a ripe almond or pomegranate (depending on the region that told it) in her bosom. He died, either being killed by a wild boar, the symbol of winter, or castrated himself like his own male priests, but he (Attis) bled to death at the foot of a pine tree. The sacrifice of his shed blood renewed the fertility of the earth. In the ritual celebration of death and resurrection, his effigy was fastened to the trunk of a pine tree (Compared to Crucifixion). The worship of Attis (aka Mithras) was prevalent and was specifically honored by military commanders of the time. Mithraism (sun worship) was ultimately incorporated with the established religion at Rome somewhere about the commencement of Roman Catholicism.

Lastly, Krishna, the Hindu god, is also in agreement with the general divine career indicated insofar. These points of agreement are too important to be overlooked and too numerous to be fully recorded. Krishna was born of the Virgin (Devaki) in a Cave,[8] and a unique star announced his birth. Leaders sought to destroy him, and for that purpose, the leaders ordered a massacre of infants at the time of his delivery. Krishna performed many miracles, including raising the dead, healing lepers, and the deaf and the blind, and championing the poor and oppressed. He also had a beloved disciple named Arjuna, before whom he was transfigured.[9]

His death is told differently; he is either being shot by an arrow or crucified on a tree, depending on the region wherein you hear the story. Regardless, he also descended into hell; and rose from the dead to ascend into heaven in the sight of many people. He, too, will return at the last day to be the judge of humanity.

The preceding origins are a mere snapshot of the many legends concerning pre-Christian deities. If you are a Bible student, you will quickly identify the themes of the virgin birth, death, burial, and resurrection of a savior contained within them all. Early church fathers were fully aware of the many similarities of such traditions, and having no way to explain them, they just blamed the Devil. They claimed the Devil had caused people to adopt such beliefs, centuries before Christ was on the earth. They also lumped Judaism in with other such cults, so a seething disgust for all things Jewish entered the church as early as the late second century, which we'll delve into in later chapters.

Famed early church scholar Justin Martyr, for example, describes the institution of the Lord's Supper as narrated in the Gospels and then goes on to say: "*Which the wicked dev-*

ils have IMITATED in the mysteries of Mithras, commanding the same thing to be done. For, that bread and a cup of water are placed with certain incantations in the mystic rites of one who is being initiated you either know or can learn." [10] Tertullian, a Latin scholar and the first to use the word trinity when referencing the God-head, also says that *"...the devil by the mysteries of his idols imitates even the main part of the divine mysteries."*[11] *"He baptizes his worshippers in water and makes them believe that this purifies them from their crimes. Mithras sets his mark on the forehead of his soldiers; he celebrates the oblation of bread; he offers an image of the resurrection and presents at once the crown and the sword; limits his chief priest to a single marriage; he even has his virgins and ascetics."*[12]

The explorer Cortez, too, complained that the Devil had taught the Mexicans the same things God had led to Christendom. The issue, however, was that Roman Catholicism had adopted the practices of these pagan religions; it was not the other way around!

Justin Martyr, in the Dialogue with Trypho, says that the birth in the Stable was the prototype of the birth of Mithras in the Cave of Zoroastrianism; and boasts that Christ was born when the Sun takes its birth in the Augean Stable, coming as a second Hercules to cleanse a foul world.[13] St. Augustine said, "We hold this (Christmas) day holy, not like the pagans because of the birth of the Sun, but because of the birth of him who made it [the sun]." The Catholics believed this because the Catholic birthplace of Jesus is located in a cave.

Having a slightly better grasp of the pervasive pagan influence over the early church, why is it that Paganism has influenced Christianity to such a degree? Is it because Christianity is just another made-up pagan cult? Perish the thought! As noted earlier, the early church fathers strayed from their Jewish Roots and attempted to hold a council (Nicaea) without any input from Jewish (Messianic Jews, Essenes, Nazarenes) brothers. Had the early church fathers had any proper understanding of the Torah (Old Testament), they would have concluded that the pagan influences had nothing in common with the true Gospel of the Jewish Jesus.

Today, however, we have grown up in a faith built upon the foundation of diverse beliefs, those of Paganism- Romanized Christianity- and Pseudo-Judaism. The first established "Christian" (and I use that term loosely) religion was Roman Catholicism. Then 1200 years later came the Protestant Reformation. The Reformation led to splinter groups forming over time, such as (in no particular order) the Bohemians (Hus), Lutherans, Anglicans, Presbyterians, then we have the Methodists, Anabaptists, Baptists, etc. and we came to the twentieth century with the Pentecostals and Charismatics. While each group has been instrumental in revealing a piece of truth based on scripture, all, and I do mean all, are still based upon the liturgical and artificial traditions of the original Roman Catholic Church. The Roman Church is built upon the very bloody foundation of Paganism.

We must get back to the book of Acts where the church began! Jesus trained the faithful church elders while He was here in the flesh, then He sent His Holy Spirit to continue teaching them and those to come until He returns in His Kingdom. If any denominational group would have looked to the scriptures and done what they said to do, instead of what had been done before (James 1:22), the church today would be functioning much more like the original congregation in the Book of Acts. The modern church would be set apart from the world instead of being intimately involved with it.

Chapter 2

The Origins of Easter

Contrary to what you may have learned your entire Christian life, the story of Easter does not begin with the resurrection of Jesus Christ but starts in the book of Genesis. In ancient times, a man called Nimrod was the grandson of Noah's son Ham. Ham's son Cush married a woman named Semiramis. Cush and Semiramis had a son called Nimrod. After his father's death, Cush, Nimrod married his mother and became a powerful King.[1] The Bible tells of this man, Nimrod, in Genesis 10:8-10 as follows: *"And Cush begat Nimrod, he began to be a mighty one in the earth. He was a mighty hunter before the Lord: wherefore it is said, even as Nimrod the mighty hunter before the Lord. And the beginning of his kingdom was Babel, and Erech, and Accad, and Calneh, in the land of Shinar."*

Nimrod became a demi-god to the people and Semiramis, his incestuous mother/wife, became the powerful Queen of the Heavens of ancient Babylon. An enemy eventually killed Nimrod, and his body was cut into pieces and sent to the various parts of his kingdom.[2] Semiramis had all of the features gathered after their dispersal because she had become pregnant with an illegitimate child; she could not find but one part of Nimrod's body. That missing part was his reproductive organ, which gave birth to the phallic symbolism that even today is implemented as a symbol of power. Semiramis claimed that Nimrod could not return to life without it and instead told the Babylonian people that Nimrod had ascended to become the sun god called "Baal". Queen Semiramis proclaimed that Baal would be present on earth in the form of a flame, whether candle or lamp, when used in worship. During her pregnancy, she began creating what is referred to as the "Babylonian Mystery Religion," wherein she proclaimed herself to be a goddess, immaculately conceived.[3] She taught that the moon was also a goddess that went through a 28-day cycle and ovulated when full and that she came down from the moon in a giant egg that fell into the Euphrates River. This event was to have happened at the time of the first full moon after the spring equinox. Semiramis became known as "Ishtar" which is pronounced "Easter", and her moon egg became known as "Ishtar's egg "[4], otherwise known as the "Easter Egg".

Easter (Ishtar), pregnant with a child, claimed that she conceived by the rays of the sun-god Baal. The son that she brought forth was called Tammuz. Tammuz was supposedly fond of the hare (a rabbit), and they became sacred in the ancient religion because Tammuz was worshipped as the only son of Baal. Like his father, Tammuz became a great hunter, exceptionally skilled with a bow and arrow as a young man, which the cults memorialized in the tale of Cupid centuries later. The day came when a wild pig killed Tammuz and Queen Easter; instead of telling the people of her son's death, she taught the people that Tammuz had gone to be with his father, Baal. The two of them would be united in the spirit of the sacred candle (Easter Candles) that adherents had to light each Spring.[5] Easter was worshipped as the "Mother of God and Queen of Heaven" after these events and continued to build her mystery religion.

The queen told the worshippers that when the wild pig killed Tammuz, some of his blood fell upon the stump of an evergreen tree, and the stump grew into a full tree overnight. This miracle made the evergreen tree sacred by the blood of Tammuz. She also proclaimed forty days of sorrow each year before the anniversary of the death of Tammuz.[6] During this time, no meat was to be eaten (lent). Worshippers were to meditate upon Baal and Tammuz's sacred mysteries and mark their heads with the sign of the cross[7] (Ash Wednesday); they also ate sacred cakes with the marking of a cross on the top (hot cross buns).[8]

Every year, on the first Sunday after the first full moon after the spring equinox, a holiday was appointed and was celebrated by gathering before the rising sun with rabbits and eggs (Sunrise Service). The festivities during this day included the sacrifices of firstborn children with eggs colored in their blood then bestowed as blessed gifts and the eating of pork (ham) because a wild pig had killed Tammuz.[9] Needless to say, the enforced regulation of a 40 day fast from meat culminated on this Sunday with wild revelry over their ability to once again consume meat and eggs.

At this point, the parallels to our modern observances of Easter should be obvious. There is a forty-day fast known as lent that ends on the first Sunday after the vernal equinox; a rabbit delivers eggs, and ham is the most popular Easter dish. The Greek historian Herodotus *"witnessed the Mystery religion and its rites in numerous countries and mentioned how Babylon was the primeval source from which ALL systems of idolatry flowed."* [10] Sir Austen Layard, British historian, traveler, and diplomat, said, "*...that we have the united testimony of sacred and profane history that idolatry originated in the area of Babylonia, the most ancient of religious systems.*" [11]

The Bible also refers to these Easter idolatries:

Judges 2:11,13 "And the children of Israel did *evil* in the sight of the Lord...And they forsook the Lord, and served Baal [Male/Christmas] and Ashtaroth [Female/ Easter]." [12]

1 Samuel 7:3-4 "*...put away* the strange gods and Ashtaroth from among you, and prepare your hearts unto the *Lord*, and *serve him only*...Then the children of Israel *did* put away Baalim [two gods/ father & son] and Ashtaroth [Easter/ Queen of Heaven], and *served the Lord only.*" [13]

Jeremiah 7:18 "The children gather wood, and the fathers kindle the fire, and the women knead *their* dough, to make cakes to the queen of heaven, and to pour out drink offerings unto other gods, that they may provoke me to anger."[14]

Ezekiel 8:14 "Then he brought me to the door of the gate of the LORD'S house which *was* toward the north; and, behold, there sat women weeping for Tammuz."[15]

Ishtar (Easter) was known by many other names throughout the ancient world. The terms used varied according to culture, dialect, and region. The Venerable Bede (672-735 CE.), a Catholic scholar, first asserted in his book *De Ratione Temporum* that Easter was named after *Eostre*, the Great Mother Goddess of the Saxon people in Northern Europe. Similarly, the "*Teutonic dawn goddess of fertility [was] known variously as Ostare, Ostara, Ostern, Eostra, Eostre, Eostur, Eastra, Eastur, Austron and Ausos.*"[16] Other names included Aphrodite from ancient Cyprus; Ashtoreth from ancient Israel; Astarté from ancient Greece; Demeter from Mycenae; Isis/ Hathor from ancient Egypt; and Kali from India.[17]

Now that you have been armed with an understanding of the ancient origins of the Easter holiday and some of the remarks against its festivities from the Bible let's now examine how the holiday began to be integrated into the Church.

Chapter 3

Easter Revolution

You may be asking yourself, "If Easter is such a bad thing, why then is it a church-sanctioned holiday?" The 11th edition of Encyclopedia Britannica's "Easter" article states, "*There is no indication of the observance of the Easter festival in the New Testament, or in the writings of the apostolic church Fathers.*" The ecclesiastical historian Socrates is quoted in the same article as he points out that neither the Lord nor His apostles enjoined the keeping of this day. He says, "*The apostles had no thought of appointing festival days, but of promoting a life of blamelessness and piety*". He attributes the observance of Easter by the church to the perpetuation of an old usage, "*just as many other customs have been established.*"[1] Early Church reformers such as Calvin and Knox protested strongly against Easter because of its pagan origins. American Christians did not widely celebrate the holiday until well after the Civil War.[2]

Knowing that church scholars have readily admitted that Easter wasn't something to be observed throughout the centuries, we continue to dig until the root of the issue is discovered. This root reveals itself shortly before the Holy Roman Empire in the early fourth century. Constantine was the Roman Emperor from 306 to 337. Upon becoming emperor, he immediately took possession of Britain, Gaul, and Spain and Master of Italy by 312. Constantine ruled over the Western Empire of Rome while Licinius ruled over the Eastern boundaries. War broke out between the East and West in 314 and 323. Licinius was killed in 323 and Constantine became sole lord of the entire Roman Empire.[3] Constantine was a follower of Mithras, the Persian sun god whose tales are also rooted in the Babylonian Religious cult. Catholic tradition tells us that Constantine was converted to Christianity suddenly and by a miracle. One evening during the battle with Maxentius upon the Milvian Bridge.

Constantine saw a radiant cross appearing in the heavens, with the inscription illuminating the Chi-Rho (The first two letters of Christ in Greek), *"By this, thou shalt conquer."* Eusebius first mention this cross in the sky in his De Vita Constantini, written after the emperor's death. This miracle has been defended by Roman-Catholic historians and Cardinal Dr. Newman,[4] but cannot stand the test of critical examination. Constantine may have seen some sign in the sky, but what convinced him was Christianity's superior claims to the most robust rising religion. Still, his conversion was a change of policy rather than of moral character. Long after that event, he murdered his son, his second wife, several of his relatives, and some of his most intimate friends.[5] Concerning Christianity, he retained the office and title of Pontifex Maximus (Pope)[6] to his last day and did not receive Catholic baptism until he felt death upon him. He kept Pagans in the highest positions in his immediate surroundings and forbade everything that might look like Christianity's encroachment upon Paganism.[7]

All the while, Christianity kept gaining popularity among the people of the Empire, so much so that the Roman population began to notice the crowds of people who stopped taking part in the sacrifices to the Emperor, Roman holidays, and other events pagan religions.[8] Additionally, the Christian differences with the Jewish people began to be recognized and capitalized upon by the younger Christian converts and the proponents of the Christian movement within the Empire. In Constantine's second edict regarding the Christians (Milan, 313), he granted them the freedom to worship and the recognition of the State. He also gave reparations for previously incurred losses, such as men who worked on the galleys or in the mines were called home, and confiscated estates were restored. A series of edicts of 315, 316, 319, 321, and 323 completed this revolution. For the first time in history, it paid to be a Christian.

Some Christians were admitted to the offices of the State both military and civil. Christian clergy was exempt from all municipal burdens, as were the Pagan priests; the Emporer also facilitated the emancipation of Christian slaves. Jews were forbidden to keep Christian slaves. A 321 edict ordered Sunday to be celebrated by the cessation of all work in public. Once Constantine became the master of the entire empire, all these edicts were extended to the entirety of the realm regardless of previous practice. The

Roman world assumed the aspect of a Christian-run state. One thing, however, annoyed the emperor very much, the clashes of the Christians, their perpetual quarrels about doctrines, and the fanatical hatred of the imposed religious rules of the State.[9]

To Constantine, the Christian teaching of death, burial, and resurrection of the son of a god matched his own Mithraic beliefs. So, the effort of Constantine to integrate the Christian faith into society as another peaceful way to the gods was, in the eyes of polytheistic Rome, a great idea. However, the faithful followers of The Way rejected it[10]; this is because they practiced a form of 'completed Judaism,' one in which Jesus had fulfilled the Law of Moses as the long-awaited Messiah. The early Christians had continued to meet in the Synagogue wherein they were welcome; they continued to meet on the Biblical Sabbath Day (Saturday), and they continued to celebrate the Biblical Feast Days[11]; the Gentile converts to this Judeo-Christian system also learned to live according to these same standards (Acts 15).

The Romans had no concern over Jewish or Christian practices on their own; Rome's steadfast dedication to their traditions would lead to problems. The relationship of early Christianity to Judaism, deeply rooted in a people accustomed to religious intolerance, helped Christianity take hold initially. The Jews were used to resisting political authority to practice their religion, and the transition to Christianity among these people helped foster this sense of resistance against the state. To the Romans, Christians were a strange community. They met in catacombs, sewers, and dark alleys, done only for their safety, but perpetuating the idea that the religion was shameful and secretive. The idea of breaking bread originating with the Last Supper (Passover), partaking of the blood and body of Christ during a meal, which later came to be known as Communion, was taken literally by the Romans. The Romans took religious custom literally as dictated by their ancient practices. So, the idea of eating the body and drinking the blood of a deity was scorned as cannibalism. The early church had to endure many such misunderstandings.[12]

However, for political reasons, unity and harmony were necessary; and in 325, the Emperor convened the first great ecumenical council at Nicaea to settle the controversies. At the Council of Nicaea, all the Churches agreed that Easter would become the Christian Passover and observed on the Sunday following the first full moon after the vernal equinox[13]. In addition to this enforced recognition of the resurrection, Constantine himself had established other laws, one being the infamous "Blue Law."[14]

Here is the text of Constantine's Sunday Law Decree: "*Let all judges and townspeople and occupations of all trades rest on the Venerable Day of the Sun [Sunday]; nevertheless, let those who are situated in the rural districts freely and with full liberty attend to the cultivation of the fields, because it frequently happens that no other day may be so fitting for plowing grains or trenching vineyards, lest at the time the advantage of the moment granted by the provision of heaven be lost. Given on the Nones [seventh] of March, Crispus and Constantine being consuls, each of them, for the second time.*"[15]

Constantine meant for these State laws and the Church Council of Nicaea to unite all contending religions into a conglomerate state-run religion. Following the ruling of Nicaea, Constantine issued an imperial order commanding all Christians everywhere to obey the decree of this council. Church and State had officially united, and whenever in history this has happened, persecution of religious dissenters has generally followed.

Eusebius, Bishop of Caesarea (270-338), generally considered to be Constantine's outstanding flatterer in the church, made this remarkable statement: "*All things whatsoever it was the duty to do on the [Seventh day] Sabbath, these we [the church] have transferred to the Lord's Day [Sunday].*"[16] From A.D. 350 onward, the persecution of Jewish-Christians by their so-called fellow Christians began; thus, the peace under the reign of Constantine was short-lived and riddled with controversies. Not only was the Sabbath day changed from the seventh day (Saturday) to the first day of the week (Sunday), but the church enforced special holidays under the rule of Constantine to maintain the status quo.

Chapter 4

Rites of Passage

Gerald L. Berry, author of "*Religions of the World*," wrote: "*About 200 B.C., mystery cults began to appear in Rome just as they had earlier in Greece. Most notable was the Cybele cult centered on Vatican hill. Associated with the Cybele cult was her lover, Attis (Tammuz, Osiris, Dionysus under a new name). He was a god of vegetation, born of a virgin. He died and was reborn annually and his festival began as a day of blood on Black Friday and culminated after three days in a day of rejoicing over his* resurrection."[1]

The ecclesiastical historian Socrates Scholasticus (b. 380) attributes the observance of Easter by the church to the perpetuation of local customs, "*just as many other customs have been established*," stating that neither Jesus nor his apostles enjoined the keeping of this or any other [Christian] festival.[2] The Easter festival is kept in many different ways among Western Christians. The traditional, liturgical observation of Easter, as practiced among Roman

Catholics and some Lutherans and Anglicans, begins with Lent and crescendos upon the night of Holy Saturday with the Easter Vigil. This liturgy is the most important of the year. It begins in total darkness with the blessing of the Easter fire, the lighting of the large Paschal candle, and the Exsultet or Easter Proclamation chanting attributed to Saint Ambrose of Milan.[3]

This service climaxes with the singing of the Alleluia and the proclamation of the gospel of the resurrection. A priest may preach a sermon after the gospel. Then the focus moves from the pulpit to the font. Anciently, Easter was considered the best time to receive baptism. This practice is alive in Roman Catholicism, as it is when new members are initiated into the Church; this is also a widespread practice within Protestant denominations. Whether there are baptisms or not, it is traditional for the congregation to renew the vows of their faith. This act of profession is often sealed by the sprinkling of the community with holy water from the font or with prayers or 'rededicating' oneself within Protestant denominations.[4]

The reason rededications and baptisms are so popular this time of year is that, during this annual feast in Rome, the pagan priests would rise early in the morning and attempt to impregnate the temple-women of the sun god with the holy seed. After this morning ritual around the sunrise service, the priests would sacrifice the babies born from the previous year's festival on the Easter altar. Eggs would then be colored in the blood of the sacrificed babes and given as peace offerings and gifts, bestowing a blessing from the gods, and the blood would be flicked over the people from a bucket just as the Pope or a Catholic Priest would use to flick holy water over a crowd.[5]

The following illustration is of a Dagonic priest, a follower of Dagon (dag=fish, on=sun). The most common way of depicting Dagon as described by the archaeologist Layard, *"The Head of the fish formed the mitre above that of a man, while its scaly, fish-like tail fell as a cloak behind, leaving the human limbs and feet exposed."*[6] This imagery is typical among all the variants of the Babylonian Mystery Religions throughout the world's nations. This imagery is also congruent with modern Catholic practices, as we see in the second image, representing the fish-head mitre as worn by the Pope and other Orthodox priests.

The Fishhead Mitre of the Pagan High
Priest (Pontifex Maximus)

The sacrament of Confirmation is celebrated at the Easter Vigil, which concludes with the celebration of the Eucharist and Holy Communion. The Priest may offer other celebrations on Easter Sunday itself. Still, some churches prefer to keep this vigil very early on Sunday morning (post-dawn) instead of Saturday night (pre-dawn) to reflect the gospel account of the women coming to the tomb at dawn on the first day of the week.

In his book, "*The Development of the Christian Doctrine*", Cardinal John Henry Newman states: *"The use of temples [church buildings], and such dedicated to particular saints, and ornamented on occasions with branches of trees [Christmas trees, holly, and wreaths]; incense, lamps, and candles; votive offerings on recovery from illness; holy water; asylums; holydays and seasons, the use of calendars, processions, blessings on the fields; sacerdotal vestments, the tonsure, the ring in marriage, turning to the East, images at a later date, the ecclesiastical chant, and the Kyrie Eleison, are all of pagan origin, and sanctified by their adoption into the Church."*

That's right; the Easter Pageants, decorations, and other things from the pulpit to the altar, from the shape of the building to the steeple, and everything in between our current churches is of pagan origin. And while Protestant denominations often refute any association with the Catholic Church, they often call its followers "unsaved"; they too blindly accept their 'sanctification' of pagan rites as valid. They, too, celebrate the same feast days as though Jesus himself appointed them, and they too are as deceived as those they seek to save. So be of good cheer, for the Lord has called you to learn the truth and share it with others; otherwise, you would not be reading this book!

The religion of Babylon became so well integrated that Rome was called the *New Babylon*.[7] The Church did everything it could to stamp out such 'pagan' rites, but by refusing to go back to the teachings of the Torah, they had to capitulate and allow the traditions to continue with only the name of the local diety changed to some Christian saint's name.[8]

Fat Tuesday (Mardi Gras)

It's a celebration derived from the Roman 'carne levare levamen,' meaning 'take away the flesh.' Pagans believed the best way to give up 'flesh' (meat) was by filling up on it before the sundial brought on abstinence.11 Fat Tuesday has become one of the best-known Easter festivals in the United States thanks to the assistance of the Catholic Church, the government of the state of Louisiana, and the city of New Orleans. This celebration is the last day a participant has to sin it up and eat meats and drink tremendous amounts of alcohol before becoming a 'holy' Catholic for the 40-days of lent.

Ash Wednesday

At Mass on this day, worshippers receive the mark of the cross by the priest. The priest marks the forehead of each adherent with black ashes in the shape of a cross (+), which adherents will traditionally retain until washing it off after sundown. Ash Wednesday is usually observed by fasting (from meat) and repentance.[12] As previously mentioned in this book, the cross of Tammuz was marked upon the head of those in the Babylonian cult. It was during this same mandated period of mourning for his death caused by a wild pig.

Lent

The word "Lent" comes from the old English word "Lencten," which means "Spring." This observance was created by the Catholic Church around 525, under the guidance of Abbot Dionysus the Little however, this period of abstinence originated in Babylon as a preliminary to the annual day that honored the death of Tammuz. It was also observed in Egypt to honor Osiris, the son of Isis, who was the counterpart of Tammuz.

Again, when Nimrod died and became the sun god, Baal. Semiramis, his wife, had an illegitimate son called Tammuz, who she said was the son of Nimrod. She said that he was the "promised seed of the woman" (Genesis 3:15) and demanded that both her and Tammuz be worshipped as gods. He became symbolized by the golden calf (Baal/ Divine Bull). She became known as the "queen of heaven" and was the prototype from which all other goddesses came. You can see her representation in the Catholic Church's veneration of Mary. These titles can not refer to the Mary of the Bible and the mother of Jesus because nowhere in the scriptures does it talk about Mary's role in such a manner.[13] According to Babylonian tradition, when Tammuz died, his mother wept for 40 days, so much that he came back to life. This manifestation was realized as the rebirth and blooming of all vegetation, which came to symbolize his resurrection. Again, Ezekiel 8:12-14 talks about the women weeping for Tammuz, which became the 40-day Lenten period.

According to celebrated fifth-century theologian Johannes Cassianus, "Howbeit you should know, that as long as the primitive church retained its perfection unbroken, this observance of Lent did not exist".[14]

The Hot Cross Bun

The sacred bun also goes back to the Babylonian queen of heaven (Ishtar/ Easter), and a reference is found in Jeremiah 7:18, which talks about making "*cakes to the queen of heaven.*"

The Hebrew word for "cakes" is "kavvan" and is more appropriately translated as "buns." About 1500 years before Christ, cult adherents used these buns or sacred bread to worship the goddess at Athens. They were called "boun." Egyptians made buns inscribed with two horns in honor of the moon goddess, and the Greeks changed it to a cross so that it could be easily separated. The Anglo-Saxons made buns with a cross on them in honor of their goddess of light.[15]

The Sunrise Service

Ezekiel 8:16 "And he brought me into the inner court of the LORD's house, and, behold, at the door of the temple of the LORD, between the porch and the altar, were about five and twenty men, with their backs toward the temple of the LORD, and their faces toward the east; and they worshipped the sun toward the east."

As we've already discovered, the sunrise service originated within the Babylonian mystery cult. It developed over time as an overtly invasive sexual invasion of naïve followers of the sun god cults. Cult priests would impregnate young virgins as the sun rose, and those that had given birth from the previous year's invasion had the fruit of their womb sacrificed on an altar at dawn on the first Sunday after the vernal equinox. The blood from the murdered babies was collected in a basin and blessed by the priest wherein the eggs of the goddess Easter were dipped and given to followers as treats, gifts, and blessings.[9] On "Easter Sunday" these sun worshippers would arise, put on their best garments, and await the sun rising, for they believed that the sun would' dance in the heavens'. In turn, worshippers would often break out in sporadic dance in honor of the sun. [10]

In like manner, millions of Christians dress up for Sunday morning service every week, and hundreds of thousands more join them on Easter Sunday when church attendance is known to jump. Albert Pike, the Masonic Cult Reformer, wrote that all pagan religions ultimately worshipped the sun. Most Roman and many protestant cathedrals, especially those with stained glass, have a western facing entrance so the sun will rise, illuminating the sanctuary, thus embracing the mystical aspects of the sun. Whereas Synagogues were built facing East so their backs would be to the sun. We still keep the first day of the week (Sunday) as our day of worship without Biblical precedent, and the majority of us still get up early on Sunday to get dressed up and go to church every week. Remember, it all started in Babylon!

Easter Eggs

Eggs are a sacred symbol of fertility among many pagan cultures. Colored eggs were used as religious offerings during the pagan Easter season and were also used as symbols of the Goddess Easter in various cultures.16 During the rule of Caesar Augustus, Hyginus, an Egyptian who was the librarian at the Palatine library in Rome, wrote: "An egg of a great site is said to have fallen from heaven into the river Euphrates. The fishes rolled it to the bank, where the doves having settled upon it, and hatched it, and out came Venus, who afterward was called the Syrian goddess (Ishtar)." This writing demonstrates the pervasive pagan origin of the Easter egg legend, though it wasn't until later that Easter was accepted as an official church holiday in 325. Pope Gregory (590-604) forbade the followers of the Catholic Church to eat eggs during Lent, so that is when they became the official treat of Easter.

The church in Poland said that the Virgin Mary dyed eggs in various colors for Jesus to play with when He was a child. The Ukrainians incorporated blue dots in the design of their eggs, which they say represent Mary's tears. They believe she took a basket of colored eggs to Pontius Pilate as a gift in hopes of convincing him to have mercy on Jesus. As she was making them, she began crying, and the tears fell on the shells, making the dots. The orthodox of Romania dyed their eggs red because they believed Mary left a basket of eggs at the cross during the crucifixion to appease the soldiers so they would treat Jesus better. The soldiers did not accept them, and Jesus' blood dripped on them. In Russia, there is a tradition that Mary Magdalene gave an egg to the Roman emperor as a symbolic token of the resurrection of Jesus.[17]

Basically, every people group on earth made up stories to explain the sinful traditions they took part in, and no priest or learned scholar ever corrected them. They flicked water over them, called them Catholic, took their money, and said they were saved. It is incredible that despite all of thigs evil that took place through the church, God continued to pour out his grace so we all would have access to Jesus and the knowledge we do today.

The Easter Ham
In the Babylonian myths, Tammuz was killed by a wild pig; therefore, it only makes sense to eat one out of revenge. Eating pork also a blatant rejection of Jewish laws regarding clean and unclean meats.[19]

The Easter Candle
As we discussed previously, Semiramis (Easter) stated that the spirit of Nimrod (Baal) and Tammuz would be one in the sacred candle fire offered up on Easter Sunday. This fire ceremony migrated into the celebrated lighting of large bonfires to commemorate spring renewal through Europe. A doll said to symbolize winter was sometimes burned, which was called "burning the Judas." This Babylonian fire ritual is still practiced within the Catholic and Protestant churches with the lighting of the Easter Vigil and Paschal Candles.

The Easter Bunny
Because Tammuz was supposedly fond of rabbits, they were chosen early on as primary imagery associated with his remembrance. In actuality, it's the hare, not the rabbit, which is Easter's main character (In America, we have more rabbits!). According to tradition, the hare was a symbolic representation of the Moon since they only came out at night. Also, the Egyptian name for the hare was "Un" (which means "open") because they are born with their eyes open, while rabbits are not. Legend has it that the hare never blinks or closes its eyes. To some pagan cultures, the Moon

was the "open-eyed watcher of the skies." The hare is associated, of course, with the goddess Easter and was her symbol of fertility because they reproduce so quickly.

There is also a Germanic tradition concerning a bird who wanted to be a rabbit. The goddess Oestre turned the bird into a rabbit who could still lay eggs and during the festival dedicated to Oestre, the rabbit would lay her colored eggs every Spring.[20] So they say, "The Easter Rabbit lays the eggs, for which reason they are hidden in a field, nest, or garden". The rabbit is a pagan symbol and has always been an emblem of sexuality.[21] This legend, of course, seems like a retelling of the ancient Babylonian story in the context of a later culture; this is the identical thing scores of pastors do every year in an attempt to justify their denominations Easter traditions. If you still are unsure about the rabbit being used as an icon of sexual symbolism, then I suggest you ask the publisher of Playboy magazine why they use a "bunny" as the logo.

Chapter 5

The Spring Festivals

Understanding that the traditions, symbols, and even the very name of Easter all stem from pagan origins, how does this affect the story of the resurrection of Jesus Christ? The Bible is clear that Jesus did live, die on a Roman cross, and rose from the dead on the third day. Still, the traditional context in which this story is told or fashioned from the pulpit isn't convincing compared with the Biblical text or historical perspective. To gain a good view of the resurrection of Jesus, we must examine the Biblical Feast days that occur in the spring of the year; Passover (Pesach), Unleavened Bread (Hag HaMatzah), and First-Fruits (Bikkurim) found in Leviticus 23.

Leviticus 23:1-14 "The LORD spoke to Moses, saying: Speak to the people and say to them: These are My fixed times, the fixed times of the LORD, which you shall proclaim as sacred occasions. On six days, work may be done, but there shall be a Sabbath of complete rest on the seventh day, a sacred occasion. You shall do no work; it shall be a Sabbath of the LORD throughout your settlements. These are the set times of the LORD, the sacred occasions, which you shall celebrate each at its appointed time: In the first month on the fourteenth day of the month, at twilight, there shall be a Passover offering to the LORD, and on the fifteenth day of that month the LORD's Feast of Unleavened Bread. You shall eat unleavened bread for seven days. On the first day, you shall celebrate a sacred occasion: you shall not work at your occupations. Seven days you shall make offerings by fire to the LORD. The seventh day shall be a sacred occasion: you shall not work at your occupations. The Lord spoke to Moses, saying: Speak to the Israelite people and say to them: When you enter the land that I am giving you and reap a harvest, you shall bring the first sheaf of your harvest to the priest. He shall elevate the sheaf before the LORD for acceptance on your behalf; the priest shall elevate it on the day after the Sabbath. On the day you elevate the sheaf, you shall offer a burnt offering to the LORD a lamb of the first year without blemish. The meal offering with it shall be of wine, a quarter of a hin. Until that very day, until you have brought the offering of your God, you shall eat no bread or parched grain or fresh ears; it is a law for all time throughout the ages in all your settlements." (JPS: Tanakh)

From this portion of the Hebrew Scriptures, we see the three spring festivals illustrated. The first important illustration is the weekly Sabbath, the seventh day of the week (Saturday). We are commanded as the people of God by birth or by grafting in (Rom. 11:19, Eph. 2:15) to obey the fourth commandment of God to remember to keep the Sabbath holy. We then see that the Passover offering must be made at twilight, the time between daytime and nighttime as the sun goes down on the 14th day of the month and that on the following day, the 15th of the month, we are to begin a seven day fast from leaven. This fast is a seven-day festival called the Feast of Unleavened Bread. On the first and last day of this fast, we observe an additional Sabbath day; these are known as High Holy Days or High Sabbaths[1] days because they may fall on a day of the week other than Saturday.

Lastly, we arrive at the Feast of First-Fruits or Bikkurim, which is the first day after the Sabbath during the Feast of Unleavened Bread. On this day, the priests gave the first fruit of the Spring harvest before the LORD for acceptance on our behalf, and the offering which the LORD required was a lamb without blemish and wine- this was to be a permanent observance. Jesus, of course, is the Lamb of God that takes away the sins of the world (John 1:29), and He has completely fulfilled the sacrificial requirements of the spring feasts, thereby becoming our perfect sacrifice once for all time (Zechariah 12:10, Psalms 22:16, Hebrews 9:28, 10:1-18).

With this understanding, let's now examine how Christ fulfilled the requirements of the spring feasts and where that leads us regarding the celebration of His resurrection. But first, how do we know that God intended for the Biblical Feasts to demonstrate His plan for humanity? One of the clues that indicate the feasts have more significance than mere tradition and remembrance is in Leviticus 23:4: *"These are the appointed times of the Lord, holy convocations which you shall proclaim at times appointed for them..."* (KJV)

The Hebrew word "miqrã'" translated as "holy convocations" also means "rehearsal". These feasts then were also appointed times of rehearsal for events that were to occur in the future.[2] Passover is the first of the spring feasts. All Jewish males were required to travel to Jerusalem for this dress rehearsal with God. The instructions for celebrating the Biblical Feasts can be found in Leviticus 23, Numbers 28-29, and Deuteronomy 16. The Passover was to be a remembrance of Israel's deliverance from Egyptian slavery. During the month of Nisan, this deliverance occurred the first Hebrew month and represented God's first encounter with his chosen people (Exodus 12:1-14, 43-48). I suggest you read the Exodus account from Egypt once more, which includes the Passover story, as we'll only be able to cover critical highlights that pertain to this text.

Every man was required to select for his household a lamb without spot or blemish. This lamb was to be chosen on the tenth day of the month, and the family was to observe this lamb for five days to make sure that there was no defect found in him. No-fault could be found in the lamb (Ex. 12:1-6). On the fifth day, the lamb was killed at the doorstep of the home, and the blood caught in a basin at the foot of the doorstep. Then, the homeowner sprinkled the blood upon the sides of the doorposts and the mantle thereof. Thus, the people covered the entire doorway to their homes in the blood (Ex. 12:7). The people made this killing of the lamb at twilight (Ex. 12:6). The Hebrew day begins in the evening just after dusk, typically around six o'clock or about an hour after sunset[3]. They would then consume the lamb the same night, leaving none left for daybreak the following morning (Ex. 12:10). In preparing the meal, no one could break a single bone. This instruction caused the meat to be roasted on a cross bar-shaped spit so that its body could be spread open.[4]

As they ate the meal, the Angel of Death passed over the land, and when he saw the blood of the lamb, he would not strike that house. Thus, the people that celebrated the first Passover were saved by the grace of God through the blood of the lamb. To see how this points to Jesus should be very apparent, but we'll continue because there is a great deal more. The Hebrew word for Passover is *Pesach*, which means *passing or skipping over* with an implication of *hopping*.[5] In a blood covenant such as this, trampling the blood underfoot meant rejection of the covenant, thus the reason for the Angel of Death hopping over the house when it encountered the blood.

At this point in history, Gentiles were not allowed to partake of the Passover feast unless they became circumcised (Ex. 12:48), circumcision being a sign of the covenant God made with Abraham. Later, when the Temple was built, people would bring their lambs to the altar in Jerusalem instead of killing them at home. During this period, the Temple became the central hub for the Passover festival. So, for 1500 years before Calvary, the Jewish people had been offering the sacrifice of an unblemished lamb unto God. They understood the blood covenant and that the blood of an animal could temporarily atone (cover) for their sins, but it could not take them away (Heb. 9:12-15). Now we can fully realize how Jesus fulfilled the Passover in His crucifixion.

In John 12:1, we find that Jesus came to Bethany six days before the Passover. Since Passover begins on the 14th, this means he arrived in Bethany on the ninth. John then described how Jesus entered Jerusalem on the tenth. *"The next day, a great multitude that had come to the feast when they heard that Jesus was coming to Jerusalem took branches of palm trees and went out to meet Him, and cried out Hosanna! Blessed is He who comes in the name of the Lord!"* (John 12:12-13). In this passage, Jesus fulfilled the requirement of the lamb to be set aside on the same day God commanded when the Israelites were in Egypt.

Now that Jesus had come to Jerusalem, he could be tested to see if He was without spot or blemish. The religious leaders questioned His authority (Matt. 21:23-27), tried to discredit Him, and do anything else they could to accuse Him of wrongdoing. Finally, on the day the lambs were to be killed, Pilate declared before the people, *"I find no fault in Him"* (John 19:4). Not only was Jesus set aside and tested for five days, proclaimed to be without fault, but He was also crucified at the same time of day the lambs were appointed to be offered in the Temple. During the Temple period, the Priests prepared Passover sacrifices at nine o'clock in the morning due to the number of sacrifices to be made. They began the killing at three o'clock to be completed by twilight around six o'clock in the evening, at which time everyone was to be in their homes consuming their Passover meal (Seder). In Mark 15:25, we see that *"...it was the third hour, and they crucified Him"*, the third hour was nine o'clock in the morning according to the Jewish reckoning of time.[6]

Mark is also careful to note that "...when the sixth hour had come, there was darkness over the whole land until the ninth hour. And at the ninth hour, Jesus cried out with a loud voice, saying, 'Eloi, Eloi, lama sabachthani?', "My God, My God, why have you forsaken me?"...verse 37 "And Jesus cried out with a loud voice, and breathed His last." (Mark 15:33-34, 37)

So as they began to nail Him to the cross, which was the spit on which the lambs had been roasted by fire (Ex.12:9), darkness covered the land. At this same time, the slaughter of the lambs began, and during the three hours of trial as by fire, he finally breathed His last, just before twilight. Additionally, we must note that the soldiers broke none of his bones following the instruction of God (Ex. 12:46, Num. 9:12, Ps. 34:20, John 19:36). Per God's instructions, those present at His crucifixion requested that the bodies of those crucified be quickly taken down from the crosses before twilight, for the next day was a High Sabbath (John 19:31). Thus Jesus, the sacrificial lamb, gave his all on the 14th of Nisan as the final Passover sacrifice, and He was put in a tomb (consumed by the world) at twilight, thereby fulfilling the Feast of Passover (1 Cor. 5:7, 1 Peter 1:18-21).

Chapter 6

The Day of Resurrection

Have you ever thought about why we're told Jesus was in the grave three days and nights, but Easter is celebrated as a Good Friday, Holy Saturday and Easter Sunday, morning resurrection? Good Friday to Easter does not add up to three days and three nights; it's only thirty-six hours! Errors like these are often cited within the Biblical texts to detract from its truth, but this is not an accurate assumption, for when one studies the original languages in which the text was written, we find that the truth is the same. Still, the language translation is what was in error.

Jesus gave the one sign that would prove that He alone was the true Messiah of Israel, and that was the sign of the prophet Jonah. *"For as Jonah was three days and three nights in the belly of a great fish, so will the Son of Man be three days and three nights in the belly of the earth"* (Matt. 12:40).

While in the belly of the earth, the tomb, Jesus was without leaven (sin) just as the people rested without sin for this period because of Sabbath restrictions. When he was placed in the tomb, the High Sabbath day of the Feast of Unleavened Bread was fast approaching. Jesus being consumed in the belly of the earth is symbolic of His sinless or unleavened life being consumed by all in the world. Again, when looking at the sign of Jonah (Matt. 12:40), whenever we see the conjunction "and" we make a connection between two or more things. Therefore, when Jesus stated three days and three nights, that completes three twenty-four-hour cycles or 72 hours. According to Edward Reingold's work, *Calendar Book, Papers and Code,* the date on which Jesus, according to calculations made utilizing astronomy, cultural context, and Torah point to only one date, Wednesday, April 3, in the year 30.[1]

If this is an accurate assessment, it means that Jesus would have resurrected at twilight on Saturday, April 6th, or the 17th of Nisan. Since the High Sabbaths were special days of rest, they did not work and remained in their homes. This assessment means that they rested on Thursday, Friday, and Saturday, which is why *"Mary Magdalene went to the tomb early, while it was still dark, and saw that the angels had already taken the stone away from the tomb."* (John 20:1) She had been cooped up in her home for three days as Jesus was cooped up in the belly of the earth- both were ready to emerge! Since Jesus was already gone when she arrived at the tomb, this could only mean that He was resurrected at sunset at the close of the weekly Sabbath. This time is the beginning of the first day of the week, the Feast of First-Fruits, April 6th/7th. First-Fruits is when the

Priests offered the first harvest of the fields to the Lord, Jesus, who was the first fruit of those to be resurrected.

Thus we put it all together:

- Wednesday (Night 1, 6:00 PM – 6:00 AM)
- Thursday (Day 1, 6:00 AM – 6:00 PM)
- Thursday (Night 2, 6:00 PM – 6:00 AM)
- Friday (Day 2, 6:00 AM – 6:00 PM)
- Friday (Night 3, 6:00 PM – 6:00 AM)
- Saturday (Day 3, 6:00 AM – 6:00 PM)

With this, we fulfill the sign of the Prophet Jonah as given to us by Jesus Himself. From this context, we see that the death, burial, and resurrection of Jesus coincides with the Spring Feast Days and fulfills their meaning, for Jesus came to meet the Torah requirements, not do away with them (Matt. 5:17-18). Why then do we hear from pulpits around the world that Jesus *'abolished the law'*? It's because of the ignorance of the cultural context of the life of Jesus and the Bible itself. Therefore, when we desire to celebrate Resurrection Day (The Festival of First Fruits), we should do so according to the Biblical guidelines, leading us into all truth and a greater level of closeness with our Messiah.

Today, when we gather together with our families on Passover, we should celebrate by getting dressed as if we're going somewhere and then recreate the Passover meal of lamb, unleavened bread, bitter herbs, and wine. Whatever food is not eaten should be burned by fire, perhaps make a fire pit and enjoy an evening outside together as the food burns up and discuss the coming week-long fast from unleavened bread.

Making unleavened bread can become a special family event among Gentile believers as it is to Jewish believers. Once you learn to examine what comes into your home, searching out the leaven (Spring cleaning), you'll get an idea of how God searches through us to seek out our leaven (sin). On the day after the Sabbath, during the Feast of Unleavened Bread, we celebrate First-Fruits, wherein we may make a unique offering to honor the Lord's resurrection.

The Lord has progressively shown my family more year by year as we've celebrated these festivals. In the past seventeen-plus years of celebrating, we understand the Spring Festivals as events with past, present, and future implications. In the past, it showed us how salvation would come. In the present, it shows us our need for Jesus, and it's only through his one-time sin offering that we can be saved. In the future, it shows us a time that we will have to run (Bug Out) because of our faith and how this event will also look (Learn more in my book *The Gospel of Survival*). God, through the power of the Holy Spirit, will show you how to celebrate the Spring Feasts and take some steps toward living a more Biblically based lifestyle. Not only can it be a great deal of fun, but it's also true- there's no substitute for walking in truth over tradition!

Chapter 7

Christmas Origins

The word "Christmas" means "Mass of Christ," or, as it came to be shortened, "Christ-Mass." This term came to the modern world from the Roman Catholic Church.[1] The Mass is the Eucharistic rite centered on the concentration of bread and wine as an actual, mystical reenactment of the sacrifice of Christ on the cross.[2] Thus, through this reenactment, the sacrifice of Christ is reoffered as often as the Mass is instituted.[3]

The 1911 edition of the Catholic Encyclopedia states the following about Christmas: *"Christmas was not among the earliest festivals of the Church . . . The first evidence of the feast is from Egypt."* *"Pagan customs centering round the January calends [the pagan calendar] gravitated to Christmas."*

Origen, an early Catholic writer, said this about celebrating birthdays in the Bible: *"In the Scriptures, no one is recorded to have kept a feast or held a great banquet on his [Christ's] birthday. It is only sinners [like Pharaoh or Herod] who make great rejoicings over the day in which they were born into this world."* [5]

The Christ-Mass is attended by the faithful, under penalty of mortal sin for not doing so. The priest offers Christ in the form of a wafer at this mass, which they teach becomes the actual flesh of Christ after being blessed; this is the Catholic doctrine of Transubstantiation. Catholic devotees are to worship this wafer as the living Christ. Vatican statements on this topic reveal: *"There should be no doubt in anyone's mind that all the faithful ought to show to this most holy sacrament [the communion wafer] the worship which is due to the true God, as has always been the custom of the Catholic Church. Nor is it to be adored any the less because it was instituted by Christ to be eaten."*[6] This Vatican II statement reaffirms the doctrinal statement made in 1648 at the Council of Trent.[7]

The "monstrance," the device that holds the wafer, is designed to look like the sun. Thus the Catholic doctrine of Transubstantiation, which centers upon the wafer as the image of worship, is nothing more than another excuse to worship an embodiment of the sun god. As we discussed earlier in this book, the worship of the sun in the middle of winter was a common pagan practice as the low winter sun was thought to be dying and through acts of worship, it may be revived for the following year.

Exodus 20:4-5 "Thou shalt not make unto thee any graven image or any likeness of anything that is in heaven above, or that is in the earth beneath, or that is in the water under the earth. Thou shalt not bow down thyself to them, nor serve them."

God's commandment is pretty plain- don't worship or serve any image or likeness of anything!

When in Rome, do as the Romans

The 25th day of December is indicated on the old Roman calendar as *'Dies Natalis Invicti Solis,' which translates as 'Day of the Birth of the Unconquered Sun.'* The Roman church adopted that date as the birthday of Jesus Christ, blending their ancient culture's pagan traditions with Judeo-Christian beliefs as a way of 'converting' souls to Christ. In reality, it was simply a way to maintain authority over the growing number of Christians in the Roman Empire. December 25th is the birthdate of a long list of deities worldwide and long predates Christian usage.[8]

However, the date of the Roman Saturnalia, a vile celebration in honor of the Roman god, is what the Roman Empire formally recognized as Christ's birthday celebration rite. The festival was initially 12 days long (the 12 days of Christmas), which began on December 20/21, the Winter Solstice, and went through to the pagan new year, January 1. The Winter Solstice to pagans is the birthday of the gods; thus, they worshiped the sun while at its lowest point; rebirth occurred after that, signified by the sun making its way back to its original point in the sky by New Year's Day.

The Encyclopedia Americana makes this clear: *"In the fifth century, the Western Church ordered it [Christ's birth] to be observed forever on the day of the old Roman feast of the birth of Sol Invictus [Invincible Sun- the sun god], as no certain knowledge of the day of Christ's birth existed."* [9]

As you may have surmised by now, Christmas also has its roots within the Babylonian Mystery Religion. The nativity's primary imagery, the "Madonna and Child," is imagery associated with the worship of the "heavenly mother", Semiramis and her son Tammuz also known by other names around the world such as Ashtoreth and Tammuz in Phoenicia, Isis, and Horus in Egypt, Aphrodite, and Eros in Greece, Venus, and Cupid in Rome[10] and Cybele and Attis in Phrygia.[11]

In the Fourth Century, the cult of the Virgin Mary arose as a result of the forceful Christian triumph under Constantine I and blossomed about 100 years later in the fifth century. The Collyridians were, according to Epiphanius in his *Panarion*: "*A heretical Christian sect which began in Thrace and, by the time he wrote in 375 AD, had spread to the whole of the area north of the Black Sea and also to Arabia*". It was mainly a female sect whose priestesses led the worship of Mary as Queen of Heaven. Their ritual was to cover a throne with a linen cloth, place bread upon it and consecrate it to Mary, and then consume the bread as a type of communion. Additionally, followers were sprinkled with the blood of a bull, which was a type of baptism into the cult[10]. The blood of a bull was used because of the ancient connection to Baal, the divine bull, which is what many of the time called Tammuz.

Epiphanius reprimanded them for their presumption because God had not given Mary any rights of blessing or baptism. His protests show the Collyridian women must have been claiming these rights. The goddess began powerfully reasserting herself in the fifth century when the feminine presence was added to Christianity by the Council of Ephesus in 431 AD when the Virgin Mary was named Theotokos, the Mother of God. Emperor Zeno rededicated the temple of Rhea at Byzantium, not to the son of a saint, but the Virgin Mary. Gradually Mary was adorned with the titles of the goddesses of old, including that of the Queen of Heaven. When the church began to suppress the goddess cults, Roman worshippers turned to the cult of the Virgin [Mary] to replace Venus. Why? Because Venus's son was also hung on a pine tree, and more ancient versions of the lineage reveal that the husband and brother of Isis, Osiris, was discovered in an evergreen. This pagan lineage is why Jesus is thought to have been crucified on a pine tree and why the evergreen is utilized at Christmas time as the centerpiece of decorum.

From this time onward, graven images (carvings, sculptures, paintings, and drawings) of Christ on the cross began to appear, specifically on a pine cross or mounted on a pine cone. Jesus had been shown in artistic renderings earlier as the Good Shepherd, an androgynous youth carrying a lamb in his arms or across his shoulders. But when the Western Empire fell to the Goths in 476 AD, the northern tribes, who were fond of the cross as a magic symbol, gave the push needed for Jesus to most typically be shown on a cross. Thus Catholic crucifixes became increasingly common and revered as a type of talisman. Once the people accepted the veneration of the Virgin, the Empire gave over the old temples and shrines devoted to goddesses to churches dedicated to Mary. The church of Santa Maria Maggiore replaced the temple of Cybele on the Esquiline hill. Another church to Santa Maria replaced the temple of Tanit, a Phoenician goddess, on the Capitoline hill. Temples to Isis near the Pantheon and Minerva (Athena) also became churches dedicated to Mary.

An edict of 754 AD from Constantinople condemns any orthodox Christian who does not: *"Confess the holy Ever-Virgin Mary, truly and properly the Mother of God, to be higher than every creature whether visible or invisible and does not with sincere faith seek her intercessions, as one having confidence in her access to our God."*

Pope John Paul II publicly prayed on December 8, 2003: *"Queen of Peace, pray for us! Our gaze is directed toward you in great fear; to you do we turn with ever-more insistent faith in these times marked by many uncertainties and fears for the present and future of our planet. Together we lift our confident and sorrowful petition to you, the first fruit of humanity redeemed by Christ, finally freed from the slavery of evil and sin: hear the cry of the pain of victims of war and so many forms of violence that bloody the earth. Clear away the darkness of sorrow and worry, of hate and vengeance. Open up our minds and hearts to faith and forgiveness!"*

Mary, Help Us Trust in God's Mercy
Franciscan Media

Additionally, the Popes have stated:

Pius IX, Ubi Primum, 1849: "For God has committed to Mary the treasury of all good things, so that everyone may know that THROUGH HER are obtained every hope, every grace, and ALL SALVATION. For this is his will, that we obtain everything through Mary."

Paul VI, Christi Matri. "The Church ... been accustomed to have recourse to that most ready intercessor, her Mother Mary ... For as St. Irenaeus says, she 'has become the cause of salvation for the whole human race"

John Paul II, Dives in Misericordia, 1980, quoting Lumen Gentium, "In fact, by being assumed into heaven she has not laid aside the office of salvation but by the manifold intercession she continues to obtain for us the grace of eternal salvation."

John Paul II again said, "Membership in the Militia means complete dedication to the Kingdom of God and to the salvation of souls through Mary Immaculate."

The Bible is again, crystal clear on this subject:
Acts 4:10-12 "Neither is there salvation in any other: for there is none other names under heaven given among men, whereby we must be saved."

Beyond the adoration of the Madonna and Child, the nativity represents the Babylonian trio of Nimrod, Great Grandson to Noah, his wife Semiramis, and their illegitimate child Tammuz. The three wise men represent the "Three Kings" which are not found in the scripture anywhere but are the stars of Orion's belt and not people at all.[12] These three stars were of significant importance to many ancient pagan traditions because Orion is known as "The Hunter" which is a symbol of Nimrod! Again, in Genesis 10 and 11, we read of how Nimrod was the world's most excellent hunter and the leader of what seemed at the time to be the entire human race. He orchestrated cities such as Babel, Asshur, Nineveh, and Calah (Genesis 10:10-12). Now, if you know any Biblical history, you'll know that these were horrid locations known for their idolatry and pagan practices.

In Babel, we know Nimrod had a Tower constructed which reached high into the heavens. We can still find this ziggurat or pyramid-like structure worldwide in Rome, London, Paris, New York, and Washington D.C. in what we call an obelisk. The obelisk represents the phallus of Nimrod. Remember, it was the phallus of Nimrod that Semiramis could not find when she collected his body parts for veneration. This symbolism may seem odd to Westerners, but the phallus symbolizes the power of those in the East. Take, for instance, this quote from Isser Harel, founder of Mossad, Israel's Intelligence Agency. When asked where terrorism would strike first in America, he responded: *"New York is a symbol of your freedom and capitalism. They will likely strike there first at your tallest building because it's your greatest fertility symbol, and a symbol of your power."*[13] This came true on September 11, 2001, when the tallest buildings in America fell. Sadly, no one learned a lesson because the new tower built in place of the twin towers is called the 'One World Trade Center,' just as it was in Babylon.

In **Ezekiel 8: 14-16**, we read:
"The angel brought me to the gate of the house of the Lord, and I beheld women weeping for Tammuz. Then he said to me; you shall see greater abominations. And he brought me into the inner court where about twenty-five men had their back to the Temple, they faced east and worshipped the sun."

So, all religious systems and practices in the world have their foundation in the Babylonian Mystery Cults, except for Judaism, the branch from which true Christianity sprouted. God called a man named Abram from Ur, a pagan nation that was involved in the Babylonian Mysteries. God asked Abram to follow him and make a covenant, to which

Abram agreed and became known as *Abraham*, which means *"One who's crossed over,"* and it was his descendants that would carry the key to understanding the one true God.

So, what is a Modern Christian to do? Jesus said in Luke 14:33, *"So likewise, whoever of you does not forsake everything he has cannot be My disciple."*

We should forsake all the traditions and practices we have that were not taught by Christ or the apostles in scripture. As it says in Jeremiah 16:19: *"...we have inherited nothing but lies and pagan gods from our forefathers."* Jesus has redeemed us from that empty life we have inherited from our families (1 Peter 1:18).

Mark 7:7-9 "And in vain they worship Me, Teaching as doctrines the commandments of men.' For laying aside the commandment of God, you hold the tradition of men-the washing of pitchers and cups and many other such things you do." He said to them, "All too well, you reject the commandment of God, that you may keep your tradition."

Galatians 4:9-11 "But now after you have known God, or rather are known by God, how *is it that* you turn again to the weak and beggarly elements, to which you desire again to be in bondage? You observe days and months and seasons and years. I am afraid for you, lest I have labored for you in vain."

The Galatians were Gentiles brought to Christ through the apostle Paul's teaching; they fell back into their old pagan worship patterns after hearing the Gospel of Truth preached. We have done the same thing! We are free of the old pagan ways and requirements. It's the legalistic pagans that demand we celebrate their days, times, and years instead of God's, this is what initially led to the integration of Christianity into the Roman Empire.

Many began to refute Rome's controlling power and began to fall away from the pagan practices, and the Empirical courts took notice. Those that still obey the patterns of ancient Rome are today secure in their paths, for they are already blind and deaf to the truth. However, those who follow the narrow way are still considered rogues and heretics by "Cultural Christians" for actually doing what God's word states.

Chapter 8

Deck the Halls

Decking the halls of our homes, places of business, churches, and yards have long been traditional staples of the American Christmas celebration. While many of these decorations are done tastefully to appeal aesthetically, some are a bit more over the top with living nativities, blazing lights, thirty-foot tall trees, and loud music; some with Christian themes and some secular. While all these things are said to bring warmth to a cold season supposedly all about family, few, if any, understand the underlying purposes of each respective decoration and tradition.

The Christmas tree
Green trees were cut down, mounted, and then decked with food offerings and precious gifts to the sun god. Evergreens symbolized immortality and fertility; thus, the reason they became the symbol of the sun god- they were the only thing that remained green. Egyptian priests taught that the evergreen tree sprang from the grave of their god

Osiris. Who, after being murdered by another god, was resurrected through the energy in an evergreen tree. Of course, the fruit of the evergreen is the pine cone, which is again symbolic of evergreen tree worship and fertility.

In Jeremiah 10: 2-4, "*Do not act like the other nations, who try to read their future in the stars. Do not be afraid of their predictions, even though other nations are terrified by them. Their ways are futile and foolish. They cut down a tree and work it with an ax. They decorate it with gold and silver and then fasten it securely with hammer and nails so it won't fall over.*"

According to *A Dictionary of Symbols* by J. E. Cirlot, the Christmas tree is also a symbol in the sense of being a pyramid: "...in European folklores... [The pyramid] is symbolic of the earth in its maternal aspect. Moreover, pyramids with Christmas decorations and lights express the twofold idea of death and immortality, both associated with the Great Mother." [1]

During the 1600's it was illegal to have a Christmas tree or Christmas service in the new land of America! Those on the American Frontier had just left the confines of the Roman religious system and were fresh off the heels of reformation in Europe. It wasn't until after the Civil War that Americans widely practiced Christmas and its traditions; this is due primarily to the influx of immigrants from the North (European nations) migrating throughout the country.

The pine cone staff is a symbol of the solar god Osiris. Osiris originated in Egypt, where he was their "Christ," who died for the good of his people and whose mother, Isis, was worshipped as the Virgin Mother. This mystery religion counterpart clearly shows that the custom of bringing in a tree and decorating it is associated with the signs of the heathen, the winter solstice in this case, and the Lord God does not want His people learning to do these things.

Jeremiah 3:13 "Only acknowledge thine iniquity, that thou hast transgressed against the LORD thy God, and hast scattered thy ways to the strangers under every green tree, and ye have not obeyed my voice, saith the LORD."

Long before the birth of Jesus Christ, evergreens were used by the pagans in their superstitious worship. In Northern Europe, they brought evergreens inside so that the woodland spirits and fairies could live with them during the winter and survive the cold. In Italy, people used evergreens to decorate in honor of Saturn. Added to this is that when Israel went into apostasy, they sacrificed under green trees, and God punished them for it.

Ezekiel 6:13 "Then shall ye know that I *am* the LORD, when their slain *men* shall be among their idols round about their altars, upon every high hill, in all the tops of the mountains, and under every green tree, and every thick oak, the place where they did offer sweet savor to all their idols."

Offering sweet savors to idols under a green tree sounds like putting milk and cookies and other gifts under a Christmas tree, doesn't it? As mentioned previously, it's also taught that Christ was crucified on a pine tree because all the other pagan deities were identified with a pine tree which represented fertility and eternity.

The Garland

The only place evergreen garland shows up in the Bible is, of course, in pagan worship.

Acts 14:12-18 *"And they called Barnabas, Jupiter; and Paul, Mercury, because he was the chief speaker. Then the priest of Jupiter, which was before their city, brought oxen and garlands unto the gates and would have made sacrifices with the people. When the apostles, Barnabas and Paul, heard of, they rent their clothes, ran in among the people, cried out, and said, Sirs, why do ye these things? We also are men of like passions with you, and preach unto you that ye should turn from these vanities unto the living God, which made heaven, and earth, and the sea, and all things that are therein: Who in times past suffered all nations to walk in their ways. Nevertheless, he left not himself without witness, in that he did good, and gave us rain from heaven, and fruitful seasons, filling our hearts with food and gladness. And with these sayings scarce restrained the people, that they had not done sacrifice unto them."*

The people believed that Paul and Barnabas were sent as emissaries of Saturn, the sun god, so they gathered the traditional decorum required to worship their God. You should also know that the statue of Peter in St. Peter's Basilica at the Vatican is a statue of Saturn that Rome brought in from the original Temple of Saturn.[2] Sadly, millions of ignorant pilgrims come to kiss the feet of this statue every year, so much so that the feet have started to wear off.

A Pilgrim at Saint Peter Enthroned
© Will van der Walt

The Mistletoe

Mistletoe is also related to pagan sun god worship. Balder, the Norse sun god, was supposed to be immune to all forms of destruction because of spells cast by the other gods. The only thing they missed in their incantations was mistletoe, and so Loki, the evil god, contrived to have Balder killed by an arrow made of mistletoe. After the other gods brought Balder back to life, the mistletoe promised never to hurt anyone again. It became the symbol of love.[3]

They also used it to cast spells, the prevalent belief that if they held it over a woman's head, she was powerless to resist, and they could then have their way with her sexually. From this comes our custom of hanging it over doorways and the tradition that if a girl is caught under the sprig of mistletoe, she may be kissed and may not resist. As it all had to do with fertility and sex, the berries on the sprig made its power more potent. Mistletoe is still considered worth more if it has berries. And if that isn't enough for you, the practice is believed to have originated with orgiastic celebrations connected with the Celtic Midsummer Eve ceremony when pagans gathered the mistletoe. During that festival, the men would kiss each other as a display of their homosexuality. The custom was later broadened to include both men and women. Balder is likened to Christ in art and pagan religious tradition. Shakespeare's Midsummer Night's Dream is in part loosely based around the Celtic ceremonies.[4]

2 Corinthians 6:17 "Wherefore come out from among them [the heathen], and be ye separate, saith the Lord, and touch not the unclean *thing*; and I will receive you..."

The Advent Wreath

Circular wreaths of evergreen branches were a featured part of the Saturnalia festival and other deity birth rites. These were formed in the sun's shape and represented a life that could not exist without sunlight. These wreaths are placed on the inside and outside walls during the celebrations. At the time of initiation into the Dionysian mysteries, these were worn by the initiates as fertility symbols upon the head. They represented the infinity of existence through ongoing cycles of life, death, and rebirth. In his book, Answers to Questions, Frederic Haskin states, "The use of Advent wreaths is believed by authorities to be traceable to the pagan customs of decorating buildings and places of worship at the feast that took place simultaneously as Christmas. The Christmas tree is from Egypt, and its origin dates from a period long anterior to the Christian era."

Today, many people utilize Advent wreaths with four candles going around the wreath. This practice perpetuates the sun wheel and couples with pagan fertility customs as the candles represent phallic worship. Advent is from the Latin "Adventus," implicitly coupled with "Redemptoris" or "the coming of the Savior," which if you have read this far, you know does not refer to the Biblical Messiah Jesus of Nazareth.

The Yule Log

The Yule Log tradition comes from Scandinavia, where the fertility god Jul (pronounced 'yule') was honored in a twelve-day celebration in December. A large, single log (generally considered to have been a phallic/male genital idol) was kept with fire against it for twelve days, a different sacrifice to Jul made in the fire on each of the twelve days. At one time, the Yule log was an entire tree, chosen and brought into the house with a lavish ceremony. Cult adherents would place the butt end into the hearth while the rest of the tree stuck out into the room. They would slowly feed the tree into the fire, and the entire process was timed to last the whole Yule season.[6]

We noted earlier how the 12 days of Christmas were derived from the original Roman Saturnalia and Babylonian Mysteries before it. Part of the old Roman Empire encompassed the northern Germanic and Celtic territories, which had migrants to the Norse settlements of Holland, Scandanavia, etc. After the Pilgrims left England, they went to the Norse settlements and remained there for about 15 years. They left due to the harsh weather conditions, but not before adopting more pagan Yule-tide customs. It was then that the Pilgrims returned to England to replenish their stock to head to the new world, America. That's how America came to learn about the 12 days of Christmas. Yuletide, meaning the turning of the sun or the winter solstice, has traditionally been a time of extreme importance in Scandinavia - a time when the gods determined fortunes for the coming year and when the dead would walk the earth. For a long time, it was considered dangerous to sleep alone on Christmas Eve. The extended family, master, and servant alike, would sleep together on a freshly spread bed of straw.[7]

In France, the Yule log is still used in the form of a log-shaped cake called "Buche de Noel." This cake has found its way into other countries, including the USA, immortalized by Little Debbie as the Swiss Cake Roll. Using logs to decorate or shape cakes after, giving yuletide greetings, and any recognition of the Twelve Days of Christmas or Twelfth night; is giving credit to this vile phallic worship of Scandinavia's past.[8] Yuletide is also observed by Wiccans today as one of their main high days, so if you are "celebrating," you are doing so with witches. The Norse also sacrificed a boar to their god Freyr during the yuletide. It is thought that this is where the English tradition of serving boar's head at "Christmas" came from and our tradition of serving "Christmas Ham"; again, it all traces back to the Book of Genesis to the Babylonian Mystery Religion of Semiramis and Tammuz.

Gift Giving

The Romans exchanged food, small statues of gods (we now give snowmen, Santa statues, Jesus statues, etc.), and trinkets to one another during the winter festival of Saturnalia. The church, adopting the customs of the heathen, declared that it was to be done officially on December 25, but in their cleverness, they deceived the masses by teaching, "the three wise men brought gifts to Christ when He was born, so we do too."[9]

Bibliotheca Sacra, volume 12, pages 153-155: "*The interchange of presents between friends is similar to characteristic of Christmas and the Saturnalia and must have been adopted by Christians from the pagans, as the admonition of Tertullian plainly shows.*"

Should we give gifts to family, friends, or to those who need them? Indeed, it is well to do this all year round, but let's not copy the heathens in doing it.

Luke 6:30-35 "*Give to everyone who asks you, and if anyone takes what belongs to you, do not demand it back. Do to others as you would have them do to you. "If you love those who love you, what credit is that to you? Even 'sinners' love those who love them. And if you do good to those who are good to you, what credit is that to you? Even 'sinners' do that. And if you lend to those from whom you expect repayment, what credit is that to you? Even 'sinners' lend to 'sinners,' expecting to be repaid in full. But love your enemies, do good to them, and lend to them without expecting to get anything back. Then your reward will be great, and you will be sons of the Most High, because he is kind to the ungrateful and wicked.*"

We should bring our choicest gifts to Christ.

"Now when Jesus was born in Bethlehem of Judea . . . and when they [the magi] came into the house, they . . . fell, and worshipped Him: and when they had opened their treasures, they presented unto Him gifts; gold, and frankincense, and myrrh." *Matthew 2:1-11*

Give Him the best you have; give Him your life. Dedicate all you have to Him to be used in His service. Read the Bible daily and obey its commands through the enabling grace of Christ. Only then can you have genuine happiness. But let not ancient paganism select the day on which you will worship God.

"Take heed to thyself, that thou be not snared by following them . . . that thou enquire not after their gods, saying, how did these nations serve their gods? Even so, will I do likewise? Thou shalt not do so unto the Lord thy God: for every abomination to the Eternal, which He hateth, have they done unto their gods." **Deuteronomy 12:30-31**

"In vain, do they worship Me, teaching for doctrines the commandments of men." **Matthew 15:9**

Chapter 9

What about Santa Claus?

While many are aware that children should not be allowed to believe in Santa Claus, some may not realize that the origins of the legend come so thoroughly from paganism, and his image and likeness are counterfeits of the God of the Bible. The name Santa Claus is believed to be a corruption of the Dutch 'Sant Nikolaas' (Sant-Ni-Klaus). Saint Nicholas (as the Roman Catholic Church canonized him) was made the Bishop of Myra in Turkey because of his reputed piety. It is told that he honored the child form of Christ and, as such, practiced the child-like virtues of meekness and humility. Legend has it that he gave help to the poor and provided his gifts anonymously. In memory of him, mothers would hide gifts for their children and tell them St. Nicholas left them. Because of his alleged piety and legends attributing 'miracles' to him, which centered on children and the bestowing of fertility upon childless couples, St. Nicholas is revered by the Roman Catholic Church as the patron saint of children.[1]

The legends of Saint Nicholas bear many similarities to those of the ancient Egyptian god Bes. Bes is a round, chubby, gnome-like personage who was the patron deity of little children. Bes was also a god of war, slaughter, music, dance, and childbirth but was also supposed to protect homes and children.[2] His symbols included bells and drums. Bes is depicted in statues and drawings as a bearded, Viking-looking, yet comical dwarf, shown full-face in images highly unusual by Egyptian artistic convention. Many texts also point to the idea that Bes was a terrible avenging deity who was just as swift to punish the wicked as he was to amuse and delight the righteous. One source claimed that Bes was Babylonian in origin.[3] Still, these and other similarities also relate to the Canaanite deity of Molech, the Moabite Chemosh, and the Chaldean Ashtaroth.

Bes relief located in Dendara, Egypt
Olaf Tausch

Santa Claus is a type of hearth god, and we find that many pagan societies have worshiped a hearth god, clad in red, that came down the chimney to bless or curse the occupants therein China's Zaowang. On December 23rd, the people living in rural areas clean out or rebuild their kitchen stoves or fireplaces as it is believed that on this day that Zaowang will return to heaven to report on the goings-on in the household. He again returns on December 30th when people stay up all night eating and celebrating, anticipating the New Year's arrival. There are other such red-clad hearth gods worshipped in India and throughout Asia today. Taiwan's hearth god is said to return to heaven to report on the affairs of men on December 24th. This act is reminiscent of the scripture regarding Israel's apostasy in these things:

Jeremiah 7:18 "The children gather wood, and the fathers kindle the fire, and the women knead *their* dough, to make cakes to the queen of heaven, and to pour out drink offerings unto other gods, that they may provoke me to anger."

Gathering wood and kindling the fires would be done after cleaning the stove or hearth of old ash. Making cakes to the "Queen of Heaven" is linked to the yuletide stollens we find this time of year, which are again phallic symbols. Lastly, pour-out drink offerings are related to eggnog and milk and cookies for "other gods". Leaving these offerings under the "Christmas tree" has even more significance again when we read:

Ezekiel 6:13 "...that they offered sweet savors to their idols under every green tree."

By this point, the connection between fertility gods and traditional holidays should be well established in your mind. So, allow me to continue to beat the proverbial dead horse just a while longer with a few more horrible facts. The name Kriss Kringle which many call Santa Claus is a corruption of the German 'Christ Kindl,' which means "Christ-child".[4] Yet another subtle blasphemy the enemy has used to infiltrate the church. As I mentioned briefly before, Chemosh, a god of the Moabites (Num. 21:29; Jer. 48:7, 13, 46), means *the destroyer* or *subduer*. This deity was the god of prosperity and is directly related to Santa Claus in a couple of ways.

Chemosh was also known as Dagon in Ninevah, the fish body god. Ninevah, of course, was founded by Nimrod, King of Babylon, who later became Baal, the divine bull. Chemosh is the masculine name for Ashtar (Ishtar/Easter) and could therefore be construed as a husband to Easter. Chemosh, like his Canaanite counterpart Molech, was an idol made of metal that could be heated hot enough to consume human flesh. It was a pot-bellied god, which is where the priests housed the fire (the belly). The priests of Chemosh wore the fish-head mitre just like those of Tammuz, Mithras, and Rome.[5]

Offering to Molech
from Bible Pictures and What They Teach Us by Charles Foster, 1897

It was on December 25th that the Moabite child-mass began. Followers would come before this pot-bellied god, now red hot with fire, and recite a list of their desires for the following year. As the cultic priests to each family's child, the good adherents to the cult's cause would have their child passed between the arms of the idol, merely being blessed by the heat. However, those families requiring much of the god would have their child placed in accepting arms of this god to be burnt alive, sacrificed by fire.[6] The coal that remained from this horrific act was collected into a bag; the parents would return home to hang the bag above their hearth as a sign of the promise of blessing on their home—the literal lump of coal in a stocking.

So often, when people hear what I have to say about Christmas, they say, "Well, it's all just for the children." The reality of what they're saying is horrific to me as they parade their children before the pot-bellied, cherry red Santa in the local mall to recite their desires for Christmas Day only to place them in his lap for judgment, just as in ancient times. Those that have been judged unworthy receive a lump of coal, reminiscent of the left over's of the Chemosh fire pit. Jesus will judge those guilty of this sort of idolatry in the holy fire of a living God- REPENT!

These are only the tip of the iceberg of the origins of the legend of Santa Claus. One must wonder why the Catholic Church felt the need to place a Saint (Nicholas) within the Christmas tradition when it was the supposed birth date of their savior. Now we know; it's because there was always a deity tied to the traditions that claimed the attributes of the one true God, so the Catholic Church had to dream up a clever way to cover it up to maintain the façade of a "Christian" institution. This mindset is something only the religious would have understood. When the traditions were taught to the masses beginning in the fourth century, things quickly took a firm hold as there was no evidence to the contrary because the church had severed its ties to the Jewish community at the Council of Nicaea. Few knew how to read, and there were no Bibles available to them even if they could do so. It was a losing battle for the vast majority of Christians in developing times.

Had it not been for the Lord Himself sending specific individuals we call "Reformers" into the world, the church would have progressed at a much slower rate, if at all. The nuggets of Biblical truth each Reformer revealed would serve as a proverbial slap in the face to the institutional man-made hierarchy, adding just enough fuel to forward the development of the church into the next age.

In one brief paragraph, the New Schaff-Herzog Encyclopedia of Religious Knowledge tells us how the Christmas holiday entered the Christian Church: "*How much the date of the festival depended upon the pagan Brumalia, following the Saturnalia, and celebrating the shortest day of the year and the 'new sun'. . . cannot be accurately determined. The pagan Saturnalia and Brumalia were too deeply entrenched in popular custom to be set aside by Christian influence . . . The pagan festival, with its riot and merrymaking, was so popular that Christians were glad of an excuse to continue its celebration with little change in spirit and manner. Christian preachers of the West and the Near East protested against the unseemly frivolity with which Christ's birthday was celebrated. Simultaneously, Christians of Mesopotamia accused their Western brethren of idolatry and sun worship of adopting as Christian this pagan festival.*"

Praise the Lord for allowing you to come to the knowledge of the truth, and praise Him for allowing you to make a change (reform) before it's too late!

Chapter 10

The Invincible Sun

By now you fully realize the Roman world was absolutely pagan, and many converts to Christianity had come to enjoy those festivities and did not want to forsake them after baptism into the Christian church. When these half-converted church members rose to leadership positions, they made policy changes in agreement with contemporary heathen customs. And that is how we got Christmas.

The 1944 edition of the Encyclopedia Americana Christmas article states: "*A feast was established in memory of this event [Christ's birth] in the fourth century. In the fifth century, the Western Church ordered it to be celebrated forever on the day of the old Roman feast of the birth of Sol, as no certain knowledge of the day of Christ's birth existed.*"[1]

If the Bible contained revealed knowledge of the day Christ was born, then we should not select a definite day to worship Him. Sol means "sun" in Latin and was another name for Mithras, the sun god who was worshiped among Roman soldiers posted throughout Arabia and Persia. Among those soldiers was Emperor Constantine, who had moved the Roman capital from Rome to Constantinople (Istanbul, Turkey). A substantial controversy arose in the Christian church over this latest apostasy by Western church leaders. As early as 354, certain Christian Romans celebrated on December 25th the Mithraic feast or birthday of the unconquered sun. The Syrians and Armenians accused the Romans of sun worship and idolatry.[2]

The planetary week wherein each day is named after a different entity in the sky, played an essential part in the worship of the sun. By the time of Christ, Mithraism most powerfully represented sun worship. Mithras was initially a deity of Iran that was worshiped as the god of strength and war by the warrior tribes of Persia. By the time of Christ, he had been transformed into the leading sun god of the ancient world and the foremost pagan god of any kind, of the civilized western world. He took the place of Appollo and Saturn primarily among the Roman prelates and military men who referred to him by the name Sol Invictus, "Invincible Sun." During the early centuries of the Christian era, Mithras was the greatest pagan rival of Christianity.

Mithraism, like all solar deities, found its origin in Babylon. The cult features a dying, rising savior, special religious suppers, a special holy day out of the weekly seven--Sun Day, initial baptism of its converts (in the blood of a slaughtered bull). Mithraism counterfeited the religion of the true God more cleverly than any other religion up to that time in history (Jude 3).

Gradually, many people began observing Sunday as the holy day in honor of Mithras. Mithras was especially liked by the Roman soldiers, for his acts of worship included athletic feats of skill and "warlike manliness".[3] The worship of the Invincible Sun became so popular and widespread that Emperor Aurelian (270-275 A.D.) made this solar cult the official religion of the Roman Empire. Flavius Vopiscus, the biographer of Aurelian, says that the priests of the Temple of the Sun at Rome were called pontiffs. They were priests of their dying-rising savior Mithras and vicegerents in religious matters next to him.[4] (Sounds like the Vatican today, right? That's because it is!)

By the middle of the second century, Christians, to avoid persecution, began keeping Sunday with the rest of the empire. According to records in Alexandria and Rome, to excuse this Sunday observance, since it was not Scriptural, they called it "the Lord's Day." Sol Invictus continued to be worshiped and was the Roman Empire's official religion until Constantine defeated Licinius in 323. After this great victory, Constantine merged the faith of the Empire with Christianity and blended the Mithraic and Babylonian Mystery religions utilizing the Hebrew Scriptures and New Testament letters. Constantine chose the scriptures of these two groups because they were the two groups most commonly causing distress for the Roman Empire.

More arguments erupted due to differences in the doctrine than at any other time in history. And, because the Mithraic priesthood did not have a written codex or tradition, only an oral tradition, it was easy to adapt the other writings since they believed their stories of the sun god shared similarities to Jesus, the son of God. By this action, the Roman Church became Universal (Catholic) in that it believed that all roads led to heaven by way of the sun god.

This sentiment is evidenced from the Pope's very mouth: *"We agree that a Jew, and this is true for believers of other religions, does not need to know or acknowledge Christ as the Son of God to be saved, if there are insurmountable impediments, of which he is not blameworthy, to preclude it. However, the fact that the Son of God entered history, made himself part of history, and is present as a reality in history, affects everyone."* [4]

This statement was made by Cardinal Joseph Ratzinger, the highest appointed teacher in the Roman Catholic Church on Doctrine. He is known as Pope Benedict XVI.

Romans 3:10-12 "As it is written: "There is no one righteous, not even one; there is no one who understands, no one who seeks God. All have turned away, they have together become worthless; no one does good, not even one."

Several years ago, WorldNetDaily published an exposé that spotlighted one of the skirmishes in our current culture war. Written by Joe Kovacs, "Christmas in America becomes battleground" reveals the pagan origins of this venerable tradition and demonstrates why increasing numbers of "Fundamentalist Christians" are realizing that one cannot "put Christ" back into something He never had anything to do with from the start.

C.S. Lewis, in his book *Mere Christianity*, asserts that one of Satan's most common ploys is to "*send error into the world in pairs*"—pairs of opposites—"and then he encourages us to spend a lot of time thinking, "*Which is the worst?*" Satan persuades us to argue over two options, or two points of view, neither one of which is true. Regardless of which side carries the argument, Satan wins the day.

In the current war over Christmas and religious symbols, Satan has pitted the secular humanists, who want to blot out Christianity and encourage almost any other form of worship, against ignorant Christians, who are fighting for the right to worship as they see fit by putting evergreen trees in schools and the right to "Keep Christ in Christmas". Atheists and agnostics are also rallied against Christ-mass bent "Christians"—for whom do we root?

The truth of the matter is that Satan is the real winner regardless of the outcome.

Jesus Christ tells us, but the hour is coming, and now is, when the true worshipers will worship the Father in *Spirit and truth*; for the Father is seeking such to worship Him. God is Spirit, and those who worship Him must worship in *Spirit and truth* (John 4:23-24); therefore, if we worship Christ in anything less than truth, you could say that we do not worship Him at all, for how could we, not knowing the truth of who He is?

Chapter 11

Prophecy Fulfilled

By now, you should know that Jesus was not born on December 25th as all the other solar deities have been. First, we must come to agree that Jesus always has been (John 1:1-2). Once we understand that, we can begin to look for the season in which Jesus came to dwell among man. To start this study, let's start with the book of Daniel. When we think of the book of Daniel, we think of a boy being thrown into the lion's den; but did you know that Daniel was around 80 years old when he was thrown in the lion's den? He had been a ruler of Babylon under Nebuchadnezzar, Belshazzar, and Darius, who was tricked into having his vice-president (Daniel) executed.[1]

When Daniel and his Jewish companions (named: Azriyah, Haniniyah, and Misha'el) were younger, they were taken away as slaves into Babylon and were given Babylonian names: Belteshazzar, Shadrack, Meshech, and Abednego, and they were trained for service in the king's court and made eunuchs (Dan. 1:1-7). Daniel interpreted one of the king's dreams and was promoted to the equivalent of the prime minister of Babylon, which made him very wealthy. The Bible also declares he was twice multiplied in wealth under the reigns of kings Belshazzar and Darius the Mede. He was appointed as overseer of the Magi or Chaldeans, a group of astronomers and intellectuals, many of whom were also Jewish captives.[2]

Did you ever wonder why Persian (Iranian) astronomers were looking for a Jewish Messiah? It doesn't make sense until you put it in its Biblical context! Daniel had many other dreams and visions over his life regarding various kingdoms that would rise and fall, but he was visited by the angel Gabriel towards the end of his life. Gabriel gave Daniel specific information regarding the Messiah's coming and instructed him to "seal up" some of this information. Thus, he shared what he received with his fellow Magi, teaching them to look for the sign of the Jewish Messiah at a specific time.[3]

Then we find that Daniel dies a eunuch in Babylon without an heir. So, what happened to his vast fortune? With a wealth so large, there would have been some account for it, and it certainly wouldn't have been left for the state. After the Jewish captivity ended in Babylon, many Jews stayed behind because they had attained a certain level of distinction. One such person is Mordechai and his niece Esther. Indeed Daniel would have delegated the reasonability of his will to trusted companions, such as the Jews that remained behind in Babylon. Now, jumping ahead roughly five hundred years, we see the treasure of Daniel reappear in the

Scriptures![4] We find that the magi have seen the sign of the Messiah in the sky above. Could it be that the same group, once trained by the prophet Daniel to look for signs in the heavens, have come to see the Messiah? For what reason would they seek Him? We'll come back to this in a moment to find out.

Ask anyone you meet, "How many wise men came to present gifts to Jesus, where did they find Him, and how was He dressed?" As you may know, the standard answer will be, "Three wise men found Jesus lying in swaddling clothes in a manger." That, however, is not what the scriptures teach! We read in the King James Version in Matthew 2:11 that an undesignated number of wise men (magi) came to the house where they found the young child, Jesus, living with His mother, Mary. In the Gospels, we find that only the shepherds arrived at the manger (Luke 2:8-20).[5] It's absurd to suggest that a group of three men traveled in the middle of winter through the desert without an armed caravan. The magi were astronomers from the east, those of the line trained by the Prophet Daniel. The same people entrusted with Daniel's treasure. Following Daniel's instruction, the astronomers watched the skies for 500 years, awaiting the Great Sign in the heavens that finally occurred on Tishri 1 and the end of the fourth millennium (Revelation 12:1-5). The constellation Bethula (Hebrew), the Virgin (Virgo), was clothed with the setting sun when the first sliver of the new moon appeared beneath her feet. In the twelve stars above her head, the planet Ha Tzadek (The Righteous [Jupiter, Latin]) came into conjunction with the star Ha Maleck (The King [Regulus, Latin]) that is between the feet of the constellation of Ariel (Hebrew [Leo, Latin]), the Lion of Judah.[6]

On the first day of the month of Tishri (September/October), on Yom Teruah, the Feast of Trumpets, this one-time celestial alignment announced the coming birth of the Melchizadek, the King of Righteousness of the Tribe of Judah. He, of course, is Jesus the Messiah (Hebrews 7:11-26). During this feast, the trumpets (shofars) are sounded, signaling the Messiah's coming, thus the astronomers (magi) left for Jerusalem. During their journey, the Messiah arrived on the fifteenth day of the seventh month on the Biblical Calendar (Tishri 15) on the first day of the Feast of Tabernacles (aka Sukkot).[7] How do we know this?

According to the Torah, men were required to live in a "sukkah" or "tabernacle" for seven days, while women were free to live in the home. However, because a Roman census has been called, men had to travel back to their homelands to be counted. So, there was an unusual amount of travel away from Jerusalem. As we read in the Gospels, Mary couldn't stay in the inn because there was no room, so she had to stay in a Sukkah (Manger/Stall is a Latin/Greek description) with Joseph.[8] She gave birth in the sukkah, and at this moment, "the word was made flesh and sukkot (or tabernacled) among us." In the King James Version, tabernacled was translated as "dwelt" among us (John 1:14). Forty days after the birth of Jesus, the law required an offering to be made. So, Mary and Joseph went to the temple but were so poor they could only afford the minimal offering of two pigeons. So, they were not yet in possession of the gold, frankincense, and myrrh as recorded in Luke 2:22-24.

A time later, about 500 years after Daniel passed, the executors of his will have brought Daniels treasure-laden caravan to the gates of Jerusalem with the proclamation, *"We have come to worship Him who is born King of the Jews."* Herod sent them to the neighboring village of Bethlehem, where the prophet Micah said the Messiah would be born (Micah 5:2). However, before Herod sent the Magi to Bethlehem, he took private counsel with them, asking them for specific information concerning the location of the Messiah.[9]

After the magi delivered Daniel's treasure to the Messiah, they were warned in a vision to depart from Israel secretly. Herod became angry that the magi ignored his request, so he ordered all male children throughout the country of Bethlehem *"two years old and under according to the time which he had diligently inquired of these wise men"* (Matthew 2:16). But by this time, Joseph and Mary with the young Jesus were well on their way to Egypt, a trip they could not have made unless the Lord set up their flight beforehand[10] (Revelation 12:1-5)! The truth is always so much more awesome than the tradition!

Chapter 12

The Fall Festivals

There are seven Biblical Holidays described in Leviticus 23. These days are not Jewish holidays as many in the church call them; they are the Lord's. They are called Feasts and Festivals interchangeably in English, but ultimately they are Moed (Hebrew) Appointed Times/ Rehearsals we as the people of God through Jesus Christ are to celebrate. We have discussed the three spring feasts which Jesus fulfilled (Passover, Unleavened Bread, and First Fruits). In the summer, there is another feast called Pentecost. Jesus fulfilled this festival by sending the Holy Spirit (Acts 2). Initially, this holiday was established to commemorate the giving of the Ten Commandments on Mt. Sinai when the fire fell on the mountain on stone tablets. In the New Testament, fulfillment of this is per the Prophet Jeremiah when he stated that in the last day's God would write his laws on tablets of flesh- thus tablets of fire (Urim and Thummim) appeared upon the heads of 120 souls in an upper room in Jerusalem. All of them began to speak forth the oracles of God as the

Spirit gave them utterance.[11] The final three feasts occur in the fall and are known as the Feast of Trumpets (Rosh Hashanah), The Day of Atonement (Yom Kippur), and the Feast of Tabernacles (Sukkot).[12] While Jesus fulfilled the fall feasts, He did it in part. When Jesus came to walk the earth, he did so as Messiah bin Joseph, the suffering servant; when He returns, He shall do so as Messiah bin David, the King.[13]

The Feast of Trumpets

On the first of Tishri, which can be in September or October depending on the year, in the autumn, the Jewish New Year called Rosh Hashanah is celebrated by the blowing of the ram's horn, also known as a shofar. The trumpets are sounded throughout the day, with the final blasts being the "*Tekiah Gedolah*" or "*Awakening Blast*," which is the last trump.[14] It is a preparation day (warning) for Yom Kippur, the Day of Atonement revealing the beginning of the *Days of Awe* or the final ten days before the Day of Atonement. This feast holds prophetic significance in that we await the return of the Messiah Jesus. In 1 Thessalonians 4:16, we read that "*The Lord himself shall descend from heaven with a shout and with the voice of the archangel and the shofar of God and the dead in Christ will rise first, then we which remain shall be gathered together with them in the open air...*" We also read in 1 Corinthians 15 that "*we shall be changed in a moment at the resurrection, at the last shofar, in the twinkling of an eye.*"[15]

Therefore, this is a day to celebrate the Biblical New Year with the blowing of the shofar with a holy expectation of the return of Jesus!

The Day of Atonement

Yom Kippur is considered the holiest day of the Biblical year, for it is the day on which atonement was made for the entire nation (Lev. 16). On this day, the High Priest entered the Holy of Holies with the sacrificial blood to atone for the people's sins. Also significant is the scapegoating theme, the goat on which the High Priest would lay his hands and transfer the people's sins. This holiday is the only day the Torah specifies as a day of fasting in repentance of sin. Jesus (Yeshua) has fulfilled this feast by becoming our High Priest, our scapegoat, and our atonement! It is a celebration of the meaning of Jesus fulfilling the Biblical definition of Priest and Sacrifice, a day of fasting and prayer for Israel, and a day to examine ourselves and turn from sin (1 Cor. 11:28, 1 John 1:8-9).[16]

The Feast of Tabernacles

If you're going to celebrate the earthly birthday of Jesus, this is the time to do so and in a way God desires. As we've already discussed, the evidence points to this Feast as the actual birth period of Jesus as a fleshly man. During this eight-day festival, the people of Israel dwelling in tents (booths) recall their wilderness wanderings where they had little in the way of possessions, permanent homes, and natural provision for food. God supernaturally provided, and when they had almost nothing, God provided again! Security was not to be found in the wealth of possession, and we, as Israel of old, must understand that these things do not come from our strength as people of the covenant (Duet. 8-10).

Hospitality, sharing, and the celebration of the last harvest are central themes of this Feast. The first and eighth days are days for assembly (Church). It was during the final day of this Feast, during the water pouring ceremony in the Temple courtyard, that Jesus said, "*If anyone thirsts let him come to me and drink. He who believes in me as the Scripture has said, out of his heart shall flow rivers of living water. Now he said this about the Spirit...*" (John 7:37-39). We know from the description of Sukkot in the Talmud that this was the exact day on which the waters of libation took place.[17]

Also, during this Feast, there was dancing, songs, and music that took place. On the final day of the Feast, there was a magnificent fire lighting ceremony in the Court of Women.[18] The Temple was ablaze with glorious light- this in all probability was the context of Jesus' statement in John 8:12 "I am the light of the world." In preparing to celebrate this holiday, we are to build a tent to dwell in for the duration of the Feast. The tent or sukkah was constructed as a three-sided dwelling with an open front that would welcome visitors and the presence of God. The roof was loosely thatched so that campers could see the sky through it, so while you lay, you can look up into the heavens.

The Lord has placed in the Scriptures how He desires to be worshipped, and none of those are by the traditionally celebrated Christian Holidays. Jesus stated in Mark 4:10-12 that His disciples had been given the secrets of the Kingdom and that other people *would see but not perceive and hear but not understand*; Jesus taught in parables so only those that genuinely sought to worship Him would be able to do so (2 Tim. 2:15). For the last 1800+ years, a relative few have sought to make Him known in truth, yet billions claim to know Him intimately.

These are the same people that will say at the Day of Judgment, *"Lord, Lord, have we not prophesied in your name, have we not performed many good works? And the Lord shall say: Depart from me you workers of lawlessness, I never knew you"* (Matt. 7:23).

My friend, allow me to be completely honest. If you keep accepting man's traditions and teaching as "gospel," then you will have no place in God's Kingdom. Prayer can't save you, Church can't save you, Baptism can't save you- it's only the blood of Jesus that can save you. Remember, even the demons believe and tremble in terror (James 5), so belief is not enough- we must ACT on what we believe and what we understand the moment we come to understand it (James 2:15-20, Titus 1:16).

Chapter 13

So, What now?

"We must learn to love God more than our ideals of God."
~ Jason Hunt, Hannukah 2008

Upon investigating other holidays on the modern calendar, such as Valentine's Day, Halloween, Saint Patrick's Day, and New Year's Day, we continue to perpetuate paganism's ancient myths and customs. These customs have been ingrained in our upbringing. And, in all honesty, they are challenging to escape from due to being so interwoven into the fabric of modern society. So, shall we as Christians cave into the pressure placed upon us by our family, friends, and culture for no longer celebrating such vain customs?

Ephesians 5:16-17 *"Redeem the time, because the days are evil. Therefore do not be foolish but understand what the will of the Lord is."*

Redeem the time we have wasted in ignorance by doing what we know is right. We should train up (disciple) others in the ways of the Lord.

Ephesians 5:11 *"And have no fellowship with the unfruitful works of darkness, but rather reprove them."*

I have heard it said, *"I know it's pagan, but it's all in good fun,"* regardless of how we try and rationalize our disobedience to God- it's the most simple form of idolatry, irrespective of whether or not we understand it- God does. This idolatry is a blindspot to most, so we are admonished to study to show ourselves approved unto God (2 Tim. 2:15).

James 4:17 "Remember, it is a sin to know what you ought to do and then not do it."

Many believe that it is only the Jews that are to celebrate the "Jewish Holidays" (Biblical Feast Days) and that God somehow gave all the blessings and new holidays to the Christians in place of the Jews. This idea comes from replacement theology, and it is satanic. Additionally, the Bible never states that the feast days are "Jewish"; it specifically states that they are "The Feasts of the Lord" (Lev. 23); they are His holidays! The issues are further resolved in the book of Acts, chapter 15 vs. 20 & 29, which states the four things Gentiles are to abstain from; 1) Pollution from or Meat sacrificed unto idols, 2) fornication, 3) blood and 4) from things strangled. While these four things seem to indicate simple eating and moral issues, we'll find that the meaning is much deeper upon closer examination.

Fornication we should understand includes lust of the mind and heart, adultery, and sex out of wedlock. Blood can be avoided by eating meats that are fully cooked and by not baptizing converts in the blood of bulls or infants, a common heathen practice still practiced in modern Voodoo, Santeria, and some Pagan Festivals. Things strangled means not choking your food to death or eating animals killed by strangulation; we are to process food humanely. Now, we come to '*pollution from*' or '*meat sacrificed unto idols.*'

According to Strong's Concordance, the word pollution means '*ceremonial defilement*'; this means religiously acknowledging anything besides Christ in worship. "*Meats offered unto*" in verse 29, again according to Strong's Concordance, means "*images sacrificed unto,*" this means giving an image to an unseen deity is a sacrifice offered to said deity.

This understanding imparts a powerful truth because we have given an image of a man to Jesus. We put that image on pictures, statues, crucifixes, t-shirts, and everywhere else we can make a dollar or 'focus' our religious attention. The simple fact is we have ceremonially given an image sacrifice to an unseen deity whom we call our god- which makes it an idol.

So yes- a crucifix or picture of "Jesus" is an idol, which means you've broken the second commandment. And yes, putting up a Christmas tree in your home is classified as ceremonial defilement for your placing an object worshipped by Egyptian, Roman, Norse, and Germanic cults in your home. The Bible is clear that "*blessed are those that believe and do not see,"* we have nothing other than a vague description of Christ- certainly not enough for a painting or photo. Why? Because He knew in our ignorance, we would worship His image over Him!

And Jeremiah 10:2-4 states that the heathen would bring trees into their homes to decorate them, and their devotion was in vain (self-serving and worthless).

We have also ascribed image sacrifices to Ishtar by way of Mary and the Easter Bunny, to the Egyptian god Bes by way of Santa Claus, and to Mithras, the sun god with the Crucifix and statues of Christ, and Zeus with portraits of Christ. Thus, we are all guilty of idolatry! If we rid ourselves of idolatry, we rid ourselves of all Christian Holidays! If we can do this (which we can!), we can begin to fulfill the greatest commandment, loving God with all our heart, soul, and mind (Matthew 22:37).

Jesus said to the Samaritan woman at the well in John 4:22, *"You don't know what God you worship, but we Jews know what God we worship for salvation is of the Jews"*. The fact is until we repent of mixing paganism with the worship of the God of Israel, we are guilty of worshipping unknown gods.

Is it a sin to celebrate the Christian holidays? Yes! Will you go to hell for it? The wages of sin is death (Rom 6:23) It's time to stop heaping up for yourselves, teachers that tell your itching ears the things you want to hear (2 Tim. 4:1-4); for the truth shall make us free!

Many argue that even though these customs and images originated in pagan cults, they are not seen as, nor thought of, as pagan now. On the surface, this argument rings true. Most people don't know that the Madonna and child are imagery associated with Egypt's mother-child cult, nor do they know that Santa Claus is a demon. However, we read:

Acts 17:29-30 *"Forasmuch then as we are the offspring of God, we ought not to think that the Godhead is like unto gold, or silver, or stone, graven by art and man's device. And the times of this ignorance God winked at, but now commandeth all men everywhere to repent."*

Hebrews 13:8 *"Jesus Christ is the same yesterday and today and forever."*

Our God is immutable; that is, He is unchanging. Did you get that? Before Jesus, God may have winked at such ignorance, but now everyone must come to repentance. The following three paragraphs are from an article by Robert Heidler on "Messianic Gentiles", I believe they further solidify the information I've tried to convey throughout this text.

"Prior to the fourth century, the Church was a very "Jewish" institution. Its teachings were based on the Old Testament's understanding of God. Its cornerstone was the Jewish Messiah, Yeshua (Jesus). For most of the first century, its Bible was the Tanach, the Jewish "Old Testament." The worship of the Church was based on the Psalms, with much singing, dancing, and celebration. Churches regularly celebrated the Old Testament feasts, even as Yeshua and the apostles had.

Beginning in the fourth century, however, Church leaders, enamored with the pagan Greek philosophy of the day, attempted to purge the Church of its Jewish roots. Repeatedly, councils condemned the observances of the Biblical feasts. In their place, they substituted "Christianized" versions of pagan Greek feasts. For example, instead of celebrating Messiah's death and resurrection in the context of the Passover as the apostles had, they used the feast of the pagan fertility goddess, Ishtar -- thus the origination of the name Easter.

As we learn about the Jewish roots of our faith, we find passage after passage coming into more explicit focus, with long-hidden significance revealed. Passages that made little sense suddenly spring to life. We gain a deeper understanding of our Covenant rights and of how God desires to relate to us. Jews who come to know their Messiah are sometimes referred to as "completed" Jews. That's a good description. But I believe it's also true that when a Gentile Christian comes to know the Jewish heritage of his faith, he becomes a "completed" Gentile! Yeshua is not only the Savior of the world but the Messiah of Israel -- and our Messiah. By His grace, we have been made fellow citizens in that commonwealth. The more we know of that heritage, the richer and more complete we will be." [2]

This good news is the "one new man" (Ephesians 2:15) message. If Gentiles would come to understand that their faith in Jesus is complete of a Jewish origin, and they would reject the influences of men and pagans alike. The Gentile church would get back to its Biblical roots and once again provoke the Jew to jealousy (Romans 11:11), for we would be practicing a Torah observant form of Judaism, the same type that Jesus and His disciples practiced.

Dare to Stand Out

Most of us are by nature conformists. We tend to want to blend into the crowd and desire not to stand out as different. Most cultures teach conformity to their children early and often, and this initial training remains with them throughout their lives. Those who stray from harmony are called "black sheep" and are regarded somewhat suspiciously by "normal" people. As adults, we feel similar peer pressure, but the stakes are higher. Now it is cars, homes, memberships, investments, salaries, résumés, benefits packages, and vacation destinations—not to mention all the latest toys, gizmos, and accouterments. Not running with the in-crowd is can be just as devastating to an adult as it is to a teen; the subconscious desire to fit in is ever-present. We may call it "staying in style" or "not wanting to fall behind," but it is the same urge not to stand out as different.

However, I must give you a fair warning as giving up the traditional holidays may be one of the hardest things you do in your Christian life. You'll be standing against 1800+ years of false teaching; all of your friends and loved ones will still be celebrating these holidays, and you'll initially feel alienated from society during holiday seasons. Your family and friends will make fun of you, citing times in the past when you have celebrated their holidays, etc. You'll also be labeled a radical by your church leaders or be accused of converting to Judaism or even being legalistic. Being the black sheep isn't always easy; look at the life of Jesus and His disciples after all.

At this point, you've probably already fallen into one of three categories:

1) You're one that already shares and believes in the message of this book and has been waiting for such a text to show your friends and family you are, in fact, not crazy!

2) You are offended by this book because you so love your holiday traditions and refuse to believe evidence put in front of you.

3) You've been blown away by this revelation and are still reeling from its impact on your theology.

If you are in the first category, bless you! I've been there and done that; keep going, for your reward lies ahead and is not of this world. If you are in the third category- be encouraged, for the Lord is calling you up to the next level of intimacy with Him! If you are in the second group, seek the truth for yourself, and you'll no doubt come to the same conclusions, but should you refuse, know that your heart is rocky ground and the relationship you believe you have with God is no relationship at all.

We Christians have another ingredient to add to the mix: our calling. God's invitation to His Family complicates matters in terms of fitting into society. He has called us out of this world (John 15:19). The purpose of His invitation is to make us different! If we accept His invitation, we agree to spend the rest of our lives as the proverbial sore thumb. We are set apart from other people globally and commissioned—nay, commanded—to widen the gap!

As I hear so often from my family members, *"Well, each one has their own beliefs."*, as this is some justification for their willful ignorance, and the much-vaunted *"God knows my heart."*- statements like these demonstrate the depth of deception one has fallen. They're blind, deaf, and lost.

Notice Paul's blunt statement in Romans 12:2: *"Do not be conformed to this world, but be transformed by the renewing of your mind. . . ."* John is equally as blunt: *"Do not love the world or the things in the world. If anyone loves the world, the love of the Father is not in him"* (I John 2:15). As is James: *"Adulterers and adulteresses! Do you not know that friendship with the world is enmity with God? Whoever, therefore, wants to be a friend of the world makes himself an enemy of God"* (James 4:4). And God Himself: *"Come out of [Babylon, a type of the world], My people, lest you share in her sins, and lest you receive of her plagues"* (Revelation 18:4).

Paul's warning in II Timothy 3:12 can be discouraging: *"Yes, and all who desire to live godly in Christ Jesus will suffer persecution."* The last of Christ's Beatitudes offers some balance: *"Blessed are those who are persecuted for righteousness' sake, for theirs is the kingdom of heaven. Blessed are you when they revile and persecute you, and say all kinds of evil against you falsely for my sake. Rejoice and be exceedingly glad, for great is your reward in heaven."* (Matthew 5:10-12)

Is this reason enough to dare to be different? I genuinely believe so, for I know that we will inherit the kingdom of heaven, and I know what we are doing is true to the word of the living God and because I have come to know Him through this refining process. We're called to be peculiar people (1 Peter 2:19); what makes us different from everyone else if we celebrate the same holidays and Sabbaths as the heathen? Nothing! That's why we must separate ourselves from God.

Joshua 24:15 "But if serving the LORD seems undesirable to you, then choose *for yourselves this day whom you will serve, whether the gods your forefathers (church tradition)* served beyond the River *or the gods of the Amorites(pagans)*, in whose land you are living. *But as for me and my household, we will serve the LORD*". {Emphasis mine}

References

Introduction

1. D&C: Dilation and Curettage is a gynecological procedure performed on the female reproductive system that involves dilating the cervix and inserting instruments to remove the lining of the uterus, while the woman is under an anesthetic. Curettage is performed with a curette, a metal rod with a handle on one end, and a sharp loop on the other. It is a type of abortion, The World Health Organization recommends D&C as a method of abortion only when manual vacuum aspiration is unavailable. – *A-Z Managing Complications in Pregnancy and Childbirth by WHO*. Retrieved on February 20, 2006.
2. Except for a shoddy translation of the word Passover appearing as "Easter" in the King James Version in the book of Acts.
3. Quote from Frank Viola, author of "Pagan Christianity" regarding holidays from his website www.ptmin.org
4. Ibid

Chapter 1: Pagan Origins

1. Pagan and Christian Creeds: Their Meaning and Origin, Edward Carpenter: 1920, Public Domain
2. Ibid
3. The birth feast of Mithras was held in Rome on the 8th day before the Kalends of January, being also the day of the Circassian games, which were sacred to the Sun. (See F. Nork, Der Mystagog, Leipzig.)
4. This at any rate was reported by his later disciples (see Robertson's Pagan Christs, p. 338).
5. See Plutarch on Isis and Osiris.
6. Ancient Art and Ritual, by Jane E. Harrison, Chap. 1.
7. A discoloration caused by red earth washed by rain from the mountains, and which has been observed by modern travelers. For the whole story of Adonis and of Attis see Frazer's Golden Bough, part iv.
8. Cox's Myths of the Aryan Nations, p. 107.
9. Bhagavat Gita, ch. xi.
10. I Apol. c. 66.
11. De Praescriptione Hereticorum, c. 40; De Bapt. c. 3; De Corona, c. 15.
12. For reference to both, these examples see J. M. Robertson's Pagan Christ's, pp. 321, 322.
13. The Zodiacal sign of Capricornus, iii.

Chapter 2: Origins of Easter

1. Pagan Origins of Easter, Article by David J. Meyer, Last Trumpet Ministries
2. Ibid

3. Gerald L. Berry, "Religions of the World," Barns & Noble, 1956
4. Ibid
5. Ralph Woodrow, Babylon Mystery Religion (Riverside, California: Ralph Woodrow Evangelistic Assn., 1966)
6. "The resurrection of Tammuz [Nimrod] through Ishtar's grief [Semiramis] was dramatically represented annually in order to ensure the success of the crops and the fertility of the people... Each year men and women had to grieve with Ishtar over the death of Tammuz and celebrate the god's return, in order to win anew her favor and her benefits! [Homer W. Smith, Man and His Gods, p. 86, as cited by Woodrow, p. 157.]
7. Pagan Origins of Easter, Article by David J. Meyer, Last Trumpet Ministries
8. Controlled by the Calendar p 46, 47
1. A Rood Awakening, episode: Truth vs Tradition, Michael Rood
2. Francis X. Weiser, *Handbook of Christian Feasts and Customs* (New York: Harcourt, Brace & World, Inc., 1958), p. 211. Copyright 1952 by Francis X. Weiser.
3. Herodotus' History, Book 2, p. 109
4. King James Version of the Holy Bible
5. Ibid
6. Ibid
7. Ibid
8. Larry Boemler "*Asherah and Easter*," Biblical Archaeology Review, Vol. 18, Number 3, 1992-May/June
9. Wisconsin Evangelical Lutheran Synod Q & A Set 15, "*Why do we celebrate a festival called Easter?*"

Chapter 3: The Easter Revolution

1. Encyclopedia Britannica, 11th Edition, pub. 1911, Easter article
2. Francis X. Weiser, Handbook of Christian Feasts and Customs (New York: Harcourt, Brace & World, Inc., 1958), p. 211. Copyright 1952 by Francis X. Weiser.
3. Constantine, To the Assembly of the Saints, Eusebius, Church History 9-10
4. Two Essays on Biblical and on Ecclesiastical Miracles, 3d ed., Lond., 1873, pp. 271 sqq.
5. The Conversion of Constantine and Pagan Rome, Oxford: Clarendon, 1948
6. Pontifex Maximus by S. Gill, About.com Guide: http://ancienthistory.about.com/od/socialcustoms-dailylife/g/pontifexmaximus.htm
7. The Conversion of Constantine and Pagan Rome, Oxford: Clarendon, 1948
8. From Jesus to Christ: The First Christians, Frontline; PBS Production
9. H. Barber, "Constantine in Relation to Christianity," *Review & Expositor* 9.1 (Jan. 1912): 63-82
10. Jewish Origins of Christianity, Raymond R. Fischer, Olim Publications 2004
11. Ibid
12. Ancient Roman Empire History, Art. Christian Persecution
13. The Vatican, http://www.vatican.va/liturgical_year/easter/2003/catechism_en.html

14. A blue law, in the United States and Canada, is a type of law restricting activities or sales of goods on Sunday, which had its roots in accommodating Christian Sunday worship, although it persists to this day more as a matter of tradition.
15. *The Code of Justinian, Book 111, title 12, law 3.*
16. *Commentary on the Psalms, in Migne, Patrologia Graeca, volume 23, column 1171*

Chapter 4: Rites of Passage

1. Gerald L. Berry, "Religions of the World," Barns & Noble, (1956).
2. Encarta Encyclopedia- Origins of Easter
3. Ibid- Easter in the Western Church
4. Ibid
5. Michael J. Rood, "The Pagan-Christian Connection Exposed"
6. Layard's Babylon & Nineveh, p.343Priests
7. Easter: Its Story and Meaning by Alan Watts; Babylon, Mystery Religion, Ralph Woodrow; Calvin Tracts; Knox's History
8. Francis X. Weiser, Handbook of Christian Feasts and Customs (New York: Harcourt, Brace & World, Inc., 1958), p. 211. Copyright 1952 by Francis X. Weiser
9. Michael J. Rood, "The Pagan-Christian Connection Exposed"
10. Controlled by the Calendar p. 47, Remnant of God: Easter Section, Ezekiel 8:15-16
11. Houston Chronicle, February 21, 2001

12. Francis X. Weiser, Handbook of Christian Feasts and Customs (New York: Harcourt, Brace & World, Inc., 1958), p. 211. Copyright 1952 by Francis X. Weiser
13. On December 8, 2003, Pope John Paul II publicly prayed: "Queen of Peace, pray for us! Confess the holy Ever-Virgin Mary, truly and properly the Mother of God, to be higher than every creature whether visible or invisible, and does not with sincere faith seek her intercessions, as one having confidence in her access to our God."
14. Controlled by the Calendar p 46, 47
15. First Conference Abbot Theonas, chapter 30
16. Controlled by the Calendar p 49
17. Encyclopedia Britannica, Babylon Mystery Religion
18. Controlled by the Calendar p 45
19. *The Encyclopedia of Religion*, 1987, p 558, "Easter
20. Albert Pike, an Illuminati member, in his Masonic treatise "Morals and Dogma,"
21. Controlled by the Calendar p. 46

Chapter 5: The Spring Feast

1. Rabbi Hayim Halevy Donin, "To be a Jew", on the Responsibility of the Synagogues Today, p 188
2. Unlocking Prophecy: Jesus Fulfills the Seven Feasts of Israel, Copyright 1994 by Return to God, P.O. Box 159, Carnation, WA 98014
3. Judaism 101: Jewish Holidays, When Holidays Begin, http://www.jewfaq.org/holiday0.htm
4. Dr. Richard Booker, "Celebrating Jesus in the Biblical Feasts", p 36
5. Ibid, p 43

6. Brown, Driver, Briggs, and Gesenius. "Hebrew Lexicon entry for Pesach". "The Old Testament Hebrew Lexicon".

Chapter 6: Resurrection Day

1. Edward M. Reingold, Calendar Book, Papers, and Code, Calendrical Calculations, 3rd Edition, Cambridge University Press, 2008

Chapter 7: The Origins of Christmas

1. *Catholic Encyclopedia, 1911 ed., article: "Christmas."*
2. Webster's New World College Dictionary, 4th Edition, art. Mass
3. Ten Difference between the Reformation and Rome: http://www.reformationtheology.com/2008/12/ten_differences_between_the_re.php
4. *Catholic Encyclopedia, 1911 ed., article: "Christmas."*
5. *Catholic Encyclopedia, 11th ed., art: "Natal Day."*
6. *Vatican II: The Conciliar and Post Conciliar Documents*
7. *Session 13: Decree on the Eucharist, chap. 5, Denz 78, 1648*
8. *Edward Carpenter, Pagan & Christian Creeds: Their Origin and Meaning*
9. Francis X. Weiser, *Handbook of Christian Feasts and Customs* (New York: Harcourt, Brace & World, Inc., 1958), p. 211. Copyright 1952 by Francis X. Weiser.

10. Jack Barr, Cults, Queen of Heaven, http://prophecyarchive.com/ray/barr-family.com/godsword/queen.htm
11. H.E. Haspels, The Highlands of Phrygia, 1971, I 293 no 13, noted in Walter Burkert, Greek Religion, 1985, III.3.4, notes 17 and 18.
12. The Encyclopedia of Religion. McMillan. 1987. Vol 2. Pg 59-61
13. Chris Dolan's, Orion, retrieved Jan. 8, 2010: http://www.astro.wisc.edu/~dolan/constellations/constellations/Orion.html
14. The Final Move Beyond Iraq by Mike Evans, Interview with Isser Harel, Page 2
15. The resurrection of Tammuz [Nimrod] through Ishtar's grief [Semiramis] was dramatically represented annually in order to ensure the success of the crops and the fertility of the people... Each year men and women had to grieve with Ishtar over the death of Tammuz and celebrate the god's return, in order to win anew her favor and her benefits! [Homer W. Smith, Man and His Gods, p. 86, as cited by Woodrow, p. 157.]

Chapter 8: Deck the Halls

1. A Dictionary of Symbols, by J. E. Cirlot
2. Jordan Maxwell, "Hidden Roots of Religion" pt. 27
3. A Dictionary of Symbols, by J. E. Cirlot, p. 267
4. Masonic and Occult Symbols Illustrated; Dr. Cathy Burns; edition 9/2004
5. *Frederick J. Haskins, Answers to Questions*
6. com; www.paganwiccan.about.com "Yule"

7. Ibid
8. Ibid
9. This was something told to me by my former pastor when I first asked him about the validity of Christmas and giving gifts in December of 2003.
10. *Bibliotheca Sacra, Vol. 12, pp. 153-155.*
11. Webster's Dictionary: Incantation: A Ritual recitation of verbal charms or spells to produce a magic effect.
12. Wassailing: Woodlands Junior School, Hunt Road Tonbridge Kent TN10 4BB
13. American Heritage Dictionary, Incantation
14. For more information in Speaking in Tongues see "Tongues as of Fire" also by Dr. Jason Hunt.

Chapter 9: What about Santa Claus?

1. Pagan Claus: A look at Christian Symbols; W.J. Bethancourt, III
2. Ibid
3. H4K: Where does God fit in?Bes; Portland State University in Portland, Oregon
4. The History and Traditions of Christmas; unknown, Christmas, www.remnantofgod.org
5. Christmas, http://www.balaams-ass.com
6. Ibid
7. *New Schaff-Herzog Encyclopedia of Religious Knowledge, art: "Christmas."*

Chapter 10: The Invincible Sun

1. *Encyclopedia Americana (1944 edition), art: "Christmas."*
2. *Encyclopedia Britannica, (1946 ed), Mithra*
3. *Ibid*
4. VATICAN CITY, (ZENIT.org) - "How is it possible to explain the unique character of Christ and of the Catholic Church to a Jew or a Lutheran, a reporter asked Cardinal Joseph Ratzinger, prefect of the Vatican Congregation for the Doctrine of the Faith, during a press conference to present the "Dominus Jesus" declaration, which is concerned, precisely, with the unique and universal salvation of Christ and the Church. Cardinal Ratzinger clarified that "we are in agreement that a Jew, and this is true for believers of other religions, does not need to know or acknowledge Christ as the Son of God in order to be saved, if there are insurmountable impediments, of which he is not blameworthy, to preclude it. However, the fact that the Son of God entered history, made himself part of history, and is present as a reality in history, affects everyone."(Interview by Zenit News Agency)

Chapter 11: The True Birthday of Jesus

1-10 "The Pagan-Christian Connection Exposed" by Michael J. Rood; This is the best-simplified explanation of the birth of Yeshua that I have found in any text, I did not feel I could improve upon it, so I included the original author's commentary throughout the first ten paragraphs of this chapter.

11. Jason Hunt, *"Tongues as of Fire"*

12. Eddie Chumney, "Seven Festivals of the Messiah"

13. Rabbi Yitzhak Kaduri Confirms Jesus is the Messiah, http://www.youtube.com/watch?v=d4CZLCDRVzc

14. Richard Booker, "The Shofar", Ancient Sounds of the Messiah, p. 27

15. Dan Juster, Th.D., "Jewish Roots", p. 204

16. Ibid, p. 205

17. Ibid, p. 208

18. Ibid

About the Author

Dr. Jason Hunt is the owner and founding Instructor of Campcraft Outdoors, a softgoods manufacturing and preparedness company located in Kentucky. His survival and outdoor knowledge are backed by thousands of man-hours in the field. Jason is a frequent contributor to Backwoods Survival Guide, Prepper's Survival Guide, and various other magazines. His degrees are in church ministry, practical theology, and outdoor ministry leadership. Jason is also a wilderness emergency medicine instructor and volunteer firefighter with multiple specialty rescue qualifications. He's the author of The Gospel of Survival, Hiking the Narrow Trail, and co-author of the best-selling Bushcraft First Aid.

www.ingramcontent.com/pod-product-compliance
Lightning Source LLC
Chambersburg PA
CBHW070303010526
44108CB00039B/1711